PENGUIN BOOKS

CHARLOTTE MEW: *Co*

'The greatest living poetess' Virginia Woolf

'One who surely stands with Emily Brontë and Christina Rossetti ... many will be on the rubbish heap when Charlotte's star is at the zenith where it will remain' Siegfried Sassoon

'She has no tricks or graces. She is completely mistress of her instrument, but she does not use it for any but the most austere purpose ... All that she wrote had its quality of depth and stillness. No English poet had less pretensions, and few as genuine a claim to be in touch with the source of poetry' Humbert Wolfe, *Observer*, reviewing *The Rambling Sailor*

Charlotte Mew was born in 1869 and lived in central London all her life. The death of her father, a London architect, left her, her mother and her sister in financially reduced circumstances, with the added pressure of two mentally ill siblings living in care. Her first story was published in *The Yellow Book* in 1894, and a number of her stories, articles and poems were published in magazines and newspapers in the first two decades of the twentieth century. Her volume of poems, *The Farmer's Bride* (1915), received enthusiastic praise for its striking originality from some of the leading writers of the time, including Thomas Hardy, Virginia Woolf, Edith Sitwell and Siegfried Sassoon. A second collection, *The Rambling Sailor*, was published posthumously in 1929. In 1923 she was given a Civil List pension, on the recommendation of Hardy, John Masefield and Walter de la Mare. After her mother's death in 1923, she and her artist sister lived alone together. Charlotte Mew committed suicide in 1928, after the death of her sister.

John Newton is a Life Fellow of Clare College, where he worked for much of his life. He has taught at Warwick University, and now teaches at Boston University. He was one of the founder-editors of the *Cambridge Quarterly*.

# CHARLOTTE MEW

## *Complete Poems*

*Edited with a Preface and Notes by John Newton*

**PENGUIN BOOKS**

PENGUIN BOOKS

Published by the Penguin Group
Penguin Books Ltd, 27 Wrights Lane, London w8 5TZ, England
Penguin Putnam Inc., 375 Hudson Street, New York, New York 10014, USA
Penguin Books Australia Ltd, Ringwood, Victoria, Australia
Penguin Books Canada Ltd, 10 Alcorn Avenue, Toronto, Ontario, Canada m4v 3b2
Penguin Books India (P) Ltd, 11, Community Centre, Panchsheel Park, New Delhi – 110 017, India
Penguin Books (NZ) Ltd, Private Bag 102902, NSMC, Auckland, New Zealand
Penguin Books (South Africa) (Pty) Ltd, 5 Watkins Street, Denver Ext 4, Johannesburg 2094, South Africa

Penguin Books Ltd, Registered Offices: Harmondsworth, Middlesex, England

First published 2000
1

Set in 9.5/12.5 pt Postscript Adobe Janson
Typeset by Rowland Phototypesetting Ltd, Bury St Edmunds, Suffolk
Printed in England by Clays Ltd, St Ives plc

# Contents

*Acknowledgements*  ix
*Preface*  xi
*Table of Dates*  xv
*Further Reading*  xix
*A Note on the Text*  xxii

## Earlier Poems
'There shall be no night there'  3
*A Question*  3
*Left Behind*  4
*A Farewell*  4
*V.R.I.*  5
*To a Little Child in Death*  6
*At the Convent Gate*  7
*Song ('Oh! Sorrow, Sorrow, scarce I knew')*  8
*Not for that City*  9
*Afternoon Tea*  9
*The Little Portress*  10
*Requiescat*  11
*Péri en Mer*  13
*She was a Sinner*  13

## The Farmer's Bride (1916)
*The Farmer's Bride*  17
*Fame*  18
*The Narrow Door*  19
*The Fête*  20

# Contents

*Beside the Bed* 25
*In Nunhead Cemetery* 25
*The Pedlar* 28
*Pécheresse* 29
*The Changeling* 31
*Ken* 33
*A Quoi Bon Dire?* 36
*The Quiet House* 36
*On the Asylum Road* 39
*Jour des Morts* 39
*The Forest Road* 40
*Madeleine in Church* 42
*Exspecto Resurrectionem* 50

## The Farmer's Bride

(poems added in the second edition of 1921)

*On the Road to the Sea* 53
*The Sunlit House* 55
*The Shade-Catchers* 55
*Le Sacré-Coeur* 56
*Song ('Love Love to-day, my dear')* 57
*Saturday Market* 57
*Arracombe Wood* 59
*Sea Love* 59
*The Road to Kérity* 60
*I Have Been Through the Gates* 60
*The Cenotaph* 61

## The Wheat 65

## Other Poems

*In the Fields* 71
*From a Window* 71
*Rooms* 72
*Monsieur Qui Passe* 72
*Do Dreams Lie Deeper?* 73

*Domus Caedet Arborem* 74
*Fin de Fête* 74
*Again* 75
*Epitaph* 75
*Friend, Wherefore –?* 76
*I so liked Spring* 76
*Here Lies a Prisoner* 77
*May, 1915* 77
*June, 1915* 77
*Ne Me Tangito* 78
*Old Shepherd's Prayer* 79
*My Heart is Lame* 80
*On Youth Struck Down (From an unfinished elegy)* 80
*The Trees are Down* 81
*Smile, Death* 82
*The Rambling Sailor* 83
*The Call* 84
*Absence* 85
*To a Child in Death* 86
*Moorland Night* 87
*An Ending* 88

## *Appendix*

Four poems with the lines indented as in earlier versions
*The Fête* 91
*Saturday Market* 96
*Sea Love* 97
*May, 1915* 98

*Abbreviations* 99
*Notes* 100
*Textual Notes* 129
*Index of Titles* 139
*Index of First Lines* 141

# Acknowledgements

I must be like many other people in never having found my way to Mew's writing until Val Warner brought it back into print. On that account alone, but also on many others, I am heavily indebted to her 1981 edition, as also to her 1997 edition, to her 'New Light on Charlotte Mew' (*PN Review* 117, 1997) and to generous private communications from her. I am much indebted to Mary C. Davidow's unpublished Ph.D. thesis, 'Charlotte Mew: Biography and Criticism' (Brown University, RI, 1960) and have learnt from Penelope Fitzgerald's biography, *Charlotte Mew and her Friends* (1984). Everybody who enjoys Mew's work is indebted to Alida (Klementaski) Monro of the Poetry Bookshop, and to Harold Monro.

I must thank Malcolm Bowie for checking and improving my translations of Mew's French and Christopher Ricks for reading through the whole edition and enabling me to make a number of improvements. In a note on the 9th stanza of 'Madeleine in Church' I am indebted to the printed correspondence that followed my article about possible echoes of Mew poems in *The Waste Land*, 'Another handful of dust', *Times Literary Supplement* (28 April 1995). For much assistance I must also thank staff in the main libraries holding Mew papers – in the British Library as well as in the two Collections whose permission to cite is acknowledged below – and staff in the Boston Public Library, the Mugar Library of Boston University, the Library of the University of New Hampshire and Cambridge University Library.

When original manuscripts and typescripts in the Berg Collection and the Collection at Buffalo are either being drawn on in the texts of the poems or quoted from in the notes, they are cited with the

*Acknowledgements*

kind permission of the Berg Collection of English and American Literature in the New York Public Library (Astor, Lenox and Tilden Foundations) and of the Poetry/Rare Books Collection of the University Libraries of the State University of New York at Buffalo.

# *Preface*

There is a case for believing that Charlotte Mew has been the lost genius of the literature of England of the first half of the twentieth century. Eventually she could be recognized as one of its major figures, alongside her younger contemporaries T. S. Eliot and D. H. Lawrence. She achieves not only a fresh voice in poetry but also remarkable authority: when she does the new things she does, she thoroughly knows what she is doing and gives no sense of merely trying for them or being laborious. And her best poems have great power and significance. If she does not rival Eliot or Lawrence in some of their other kinds of success, she is probably unrivalled by either of them in tragic vision. Neither can match her bald and stark directness in the representation of the intransigent facts, particularly the facts of human isolation, of the often insurmountable divisions and distances between human beings. The depth and truth with which she handles this are not only very moving: the courage involved inspires something like awe.

If much or all of this is true, an explanation of how her work got lost is wanted. The reasons are probably many and must include the fact that Mew never collected any of her prose at all and in her life-time published only one book of poems, with a slimmer book following posthumously. But her work is also likely to have got lost for the shameful gender reason. Her main work was in poetry, but in that medium, unlike the less prestigious one of prose fiction, women had hardly ever, in Western Europe, been thought capable of equalling men. And this prejudice seems to have been even stronger after her death in 1928 than during her lifetime.

For Mew *had* succeeded in winning significant recognition from her immediate contemporaries, some of whom had seen her as a major figure. Edith Sitwell was exaggerating only a little when, in 1921, reviewing the second edition of Mew's *The Farmer's Bride*, she wrote that the 1916 first edition had been 'hailed with enthusiasm by all poets, who with one accord acclaimed it as the work of a great poet'. Some such acclaim there certainly had been, and from the people whose acclaim it is most worth a new writer's having: other writers. Thomas Hardy was one of her fellow-poets who had been strongly impressed. Later, in 1923, he was also a co-signatory with John Masefield and Walter de la Mare of a letter successfully recommending Mew for a Civil List pension and describing her as 'the most distinguished of the living women-writers'. (Hardy himself requested that the larger claim 'women-writers' replace the original 'women-poets' – so that, presumably, she was being described as more distinguished than Virginia Woolf.) In 1913, the poet and novelist May Sinclair had already written to Mew: 'I don't know any living writer (with, possibly, the exception of D. H. Lawrence) who is writing things with such profound vitality in them. And you have qualities of tenderness and subtlety that he has not.' Sinclair had shown poems to Ezra Pound, who had sent three to *Poetry* (Chicago), without result, and himself published 'The Fête' in *The Egoist*. That magazine had had an enthusiastic review of the 1916 *Farmer's Bride* by another poet, H.D. Other fellow-writers who greatly admired the poems were Virginia Woolf herself, who called Mew 'the greatest living poetess', and Siegfried Sassoon, who in 1924 wrote to Mew: '[Poets] carry the world on their shoulders, so it seems to me . . . I wish more of them were as intensely aware of their responsibility as you are, and sustained it so nobly. Forgive this effusiveness, but I feel very strongly about what you have done in verse.' A claim as high as 'the most interesting verse ever written by a woman' was made by a now forgotten poet, Margaret Sackville, reviewing the 1921 *Farmer's Bride*.

In addition, long before 1916, Mew had already won some emphatic recognition for prose stories. Henry Harland had printed one in the second number of *The Yellow Book* in 1894, and in 1895 had written warmly to her about a second story she had sent him,

'The China Bowl': 'There is no living writer of English fiction who can touch you.' To the editor of this present book the tribute seems a just one, even though Hardy and Henry James were then among the living writers of English fiction, and though not all Mew's stories are as good as 'The China Bowl'.

Not that, after the early acclaim, there were no later tributes at all to the poetry. For example, when a *Collected Poems* was published in 1953 and in the US in 1954, Marianne Moore was quoted on the American dust-jacket: 'The collection is to me extraordinary – impassioned, unforced and masterly in a technical way, almost without exception. There are in the style traces of W. B. Yeats and Thomas Hardy, but the overall effect is unique, of indigenous originality ... the work is above praise.' Nevertheless, for all too many readers of English poetry in the decades since Mew's death seventy years ago, both the poems and their writer's name have been lost.

Born in 1869, Charlotte Mew lived all her life near the centre of London, mostly in Bloomsbury but briefly, later, on the Camden Town side of Regent's Park. She also lived all her life in the family she was born into, one of two (remaining) sisters who stayed together with each other after losing their mother in 1923. When her architect father had died earlier, in 1898, the family became less well off and rented out some of their Bloomsbury house. They also had the financial burden of providing for the nursing of two other of Mew's siblings, a brother and a third sister, each confined as insane (the brother died in 1901). Though Mew earned some money by sending stories, essays and poems to magazines, she seems never to have done any other paid work, only some voluntary social work and a little work for the Poetry Bookshop.

Val Warner, Mew's most recent editor, believes that the acceptance of her story by *The Yellow Book* may have encouraged Mew to concentrate on prose for the rest of the 1890s. She is not known to have published any poems before 1901, and, though there is a possibility that at least one of her surviving poems had been written in the early 1890s, the probability is that the great majority of them were written much later, perhaps many of them in what Warner calls 'Mew's *annus mirabilis* of poetry', spring 1913 to spring 1914. If this is right, her prose stories would then more or less constitute her early work. But 'The Wheat', one of the stories she appears never to have published, is probably much later. Warner thinks it was written about 1915. It is included in the present collection of the poems not only because of its outstanding merit and its brevity but also because, unlike her longer stories, it has the concentration and intensity of a prose-poem.

The 1981 publication of Val Warner's *Charlotte Mew: Collected Poems and Prose* has been the major event in the revival of Mew's reputation. This was also the first time the prose had ever been collected. The book put into print for the first time five poems, seven stories (one unfinished), a review and the dramatized version of the story 'The China Bowl'. Sadly, it is now out of print and, with it, most of Mew's stories and essays. Only a few are in Warner's later *Charlotte Mew: Collected Poems and Selected Prose* (1997).

Finally, a dedication of my work on this edition: to another rare true poet, Joanne Weiss.

# Table of Dates

1869 *November 15*: Charlotte Mary Mew is born at 10 Doughty Street, Mecklenburgh Square, in the Bloomsbury area of central London, third of seven children and first of three daughters of Fred Mew, an architect originally from the Isle of Wight, and Anna Maria, daughter of the London architect H. E. Kendall. In the Kendall firm, Fred Mew has been an assistant and is now a junior partner. The family is to live in the Doughty Street house till 1890, and the children to have frequent summer holidays in the Isle of Wight.

1876 Two younger brothers die, one in infancy and one at the age of five. An older brother had died in infancy before Mew was born.

1879 Mew enters the Lucy Harrison School for Girls in nearby Gower Street.

1882–4 With other of the older pupils Mew boards with Lucy Harrison in the rooms in Hampstead that the latter has taken, on giving up her post as Headmistress of the school.

1885 H. E. Kendall dies, and Fred Mew is left in charge of the Kendall family firm.

1890 The Mews move from the Doughty Street house to 9 Gordon Street, also in Bloomsbury. In the late 1880s, Mew's eldest brother, Henry, shows signs of mental breakdown and ends up confined to the Peckham House Lunatic Asylum, looked after there by a private nurse. The family is now reduced to the parents and three daughters. Later, Mew's youngest sister, Freda, is also to show signs of mental breakdown, eventually becoming a patient in the Isle of Wight County Mental

Hospital where she is to die in 1958. Later still, Mew tells Alida Monro that she and her other sister Anne had vowed never to marry because of the hereditary insanity in the family. (Val Warner suggests that for Mew, though not for her sister, the real reason for renouncing marriage was her being a lesbian.)

1893 Elizabeth Goodman, the nurse to all the Mew children, who has continued to be a live-in servant with the family, dies. Mew is to write an article on her, 'An Old Servant', first published in 1913, and another on the family's needlewoman, 'Miss Bolt', first published in 1901 (both collected in Val Warner's 1981 *Charlotte Mew: Collected Poems and Prose*, the former also in her 1997 *Charlotte Mew: Collected Poems and Selected Prose*).

1894 Henry Harland accepts Mew's story 'Passed' for *The Yellow Book* and prints it in the magazine's second number. Mew meets other writers and artists by attending Harland's Saturday evenings in Cromwell Road in West London.

1895 Mew visits Cornwall and writes a story set in a Cornish fishing village: 'The China Bowl'. *The Yellow Book* is mortally damaged by the scandal of Oscar Wilde's arrest.

1898 Mew's father dies. The surviving family rents off part of the house in Gordon Street, eventually living in its basement.

1899 'The China Bowl' is printed in two parts in *Temple Bar*, a monthly that goes on to publish more of Mew's writing – poems and essays as well as stories – until it ceases publication in 1906.

1901 Mew's mentally ill eldest brother Henry dies of pneumonia, and is buried in Nunhead Cemetery in south London. Mew is one of a party of six women taking a holiday in Brittany and writes an account of it in *Temple Bar*.

1909 Mew's sister Anne, a designer and painter, takes a studio in nearby Charlotte Street.

1912 Mew's poem 'The Farmer's Bride' is printed in *The Nation*. She is taken up by Catherine Amy Dawson Scott, novelist and founder of PEN, and attends small literary gatherings in the latter's house in Southall, on the west side of London, reading her poems there and impressing listeners with the exceptional intensity and power of the readings as well as of the poems.

1913 A friendship begins with May Sinclair, who shows poems of Mew's to Ezra Pound. Mew has begun to do voluntary social work for a Girls' Club a few streets away from the house. She is to do further voluntary social work during the Great War.

1914 Pound prints Mew's poem 'The Fête' in *The Egoist*.

1915 Mew receives a letter from Alida Klementaski (later Monro), who asks whether she has poems to put together with 'The Farmer's Bride' to make a small book that could be published by Harold Monro's Poetry Bookshop. Mew begins to attend poetry-readings at the Bookshop, later helping Alida with some of the work there.

1916 Mew's collection of poems is published under the title of *The Farmer's Bride*.

1918 After Sir Sydney Cockerell, former secretary of William Morris and since 1908 Director of the Fitzwilliam Museum in Cambridge, has admired the poems and introduced Thomas Hardy (among others) to them, Mew is invited to visit Thomas and Florence Hardy and does so. A long-sustained friendship and correspondence begin with Florence Hardy.

1921 A new edition of *The Farmer's Bride* is published, with eleven additional poems, and, under the title *Saturday Market*, it is published by Macmillan in the US.

1922 The Mews move from Gordon Street, on the expiry of the lease of their house there, to 86 Delancey Street (on the Camden Town side of Regent's Park).

1923 Mew's mother dies. On Sydney Cockerell's initiative, a recommendation of Mew for a Civil List pension is made jointly by Hardy, John Masefield and Walter de la Mare, and she is granted a £75 pension. A surviving letter of Cockerell's to Mew, of November, suggests that she might have just made a first suicide attempt.

1926 The Delancey Street house is given up. Mew and her ailing sister Anne spend some weeks in Chichester and live temporarily in Anne's studio in Charlotte Street, then in rooms a few doors away from this. Anne enters a nursing-home.

1927 Anne dies of cancer.

1928 February 15: Mew enters a nursing-home at 37 Beaumont Street (near Baker Street station). March 24: she kills herself by drinking disinfectant.

1929 A new collection of Mew's poems is published by the Poetry Bookshop under the title of *The Rambling Sailor*.

# Further Reading

## BIOGRAPHY

The only published biography of Charlotte Mew is Penelope Fitzgerald's *Charlotte Mew and her Friends* (Collins, London, 1984), though Alida Monro prefaced *Collected Poems of Charlotte Mew* (Duckworth, London, 1953) with 'Charlotte Mew – A Memoir' as well as prefacing Mew's posthumous *The Rambling Sailor* (Poetry Bookshop, London, 1929) with a two-page Introductory Note. Brief biographies are included in Val Warner's Introductions to *Charlotte Mew: Collected Poems and Prose* (Carcanet, Manchester, 1981, and Virago, London, 1982) and *Charlotte Mew: Collected Poems and Selected Prose* (Carcanet, Manchester, 1997). See also Warner's 'New Light on Charlotte Mew' in *PN Review* 117, 1997. Marjorie Watts, who as a child had known Mew, published 'Memories of Charlotte Mew' in the *PEN Broadsheet* of Autumn 1982. Mary C. Davidow's unpublished Ph.D. thesis, 'Charlotte Mew: Biography and Criticism' (Brown University, RI, 1960), contains a valuable collection of letters to and from Mew. (Its biography includes the speculation, for which there is no evidence, that many years before their recorded first meeting in 1918 there had been a love-affair between Mew and Thomas Hardy and that Hardy had been portraying her in the Sue Bridehead of *Jude the Obscure*.)

## EDITIONS

The collections edited by Alida Monro (1953) and Val Warner (1981 and 1997), mentioned above, are the only collections of Mew's poems published since the Poetry Bookshop's *The Farmer's Bride* (London, 1916, 1921 and 1929) and *The Rambling Sailor* (London, 1929). The second, 1921, edition of *The Farmer's Bride*, which has eleven additional poems, was published in the US (Macmillan, New York, 1921) under the different title *Saturday Market*. The prose in Warner's *Charlotte Mew: Collected Poems and Prose* consists of stories, essays and the dramatized version of the story 'The China Bowl', and occupies over six times the number of pages that the poems occupy. In Warner's more recent *Charlotte Mew: Collected Poems and Selected Prose* there is very much less of the prose: it does not take up half of the book. A selection of Mew's poems by Christopher L. Carduff is included in the US edition of Penelope Fitzgerald's *Charlotte Mew and her Friends* (Addison-Wesley, New York, 1988).

## CRITICISM

There is discussion of Mew's poems in Fitzgerald's biography, Alida Monro's Memoir, Davidow's unpublished thesis, and Warner's Introductions (all mentioned above), and also in Warner's 'Mary Magdalene and the Bride; the work of Charlotte Mew' (*Poetry Nation*, 1975), Jeredith Merrin's 'The Ballad of Charlotte Mew' (*Modern Philology*, November 1997), Angela Leighton's chapter on Mew in her *Victorian Women Poets: Writing Against the Heart* (Harvester Wheatsheaf, London, and the University Press of Virginia, Charlottesville, 1992) and my own 'Charlotte Mew's Place in the Future of English Poetry' (*New England Review*, Spring 1997). Less favourable views of the poems than these, or than the statements quoted in the Preface to this book, can be found in Brad Leithauser's Foreword to the US edition of Fitzgerald's biography and in a 1921 review by Edgell Rickwood, reprinted in his *Essays &*

*Opinions 1921–1931*, edited by Alan Young (Carcanet, Manchester, 1974). Some recent essays on Mew's work have been marred by their writers' unthinking assumption that the work's significance must all be autobiographical – unthinking since there seems to be no consciousness of the disrespect being expressed for the poetry.

# A Note on the Text

In the present edition, fresh consultation of the original manuscripts and typescripts has led to some divergencies from the text of Val Warner's 1981 edition and her 1997 edition, as also from the texts in the original Poetry Bookshop editions of *The Farmer's Bride* and posthumous edition of *The Rambling Sailor*. The divergencies are slight. Almost all of them are only in punctuation and line-indentation, not in wording. There is a fuller statement about them in the Textual Notes.

*Earlier Poems*

### 'There shall be no night there'
In the Fields

Across these wind-blown meadows I can see
  The far off glimmer of the little town,
  And feel the darkness slowly shutting down
To lock from day's long glare my soul and me.
  Then through my blood the coming mystery
Of night steals to my heart and turns my feet
Towards that chamber in the lamp-lit street,
  Where waits the pillow of thy breast and thee.

'There shall be no night there' – no curtained pane
  To shroud love's speechlessness and loose thy hair
For kisses swift and sweet as falling rain.
  No soft release of life – no evening prayer.
  Nor shall we waking greet the dawn, aware
That with the darkness we may sleep again.


### A Question

If Christ was crucified – Ah! God, are we
  Not scourged, tormented, mocked and called to pay
  The sin of ages in our little day –
Has man no crown of thorns, no Calvary,
Though Christ has tasted of his agony?
  We knew no Eden and the poisoned fruit
  We did not pluck, yet from the bitter root
We sprang, maimed branches of iniquity.

Have we who share the heritage accurst
    Wrought nothing? Tainted to the end of time,
The last frail souls still suffer for the first
    Blind victims of an everlasting crime.
Ask of the Crucified, Who hangs enthroned,
If man – oh! God, man too has not atoned!


## Left Behind

Wilt thou have pity? intercede for me.
    So near, at last thou standest to the throne,
    Thou mayest call for mercy on thine own,
As here thine own for mercy calls on thee.
Fling then my soul, thy soul, upon its knee;
    Bestir these lips of mine for me to pray;
    Release this spirit from its tortured clay,
Remembering that thine, its mate, is free.

I wait thy summons on a swaying floor,
    Within a room half darkness and half glare.
    I cannot stir – I cannot find the stair –
      Thrust hands upon my heart –; it clogs my feet,
      As drop by drop it drains. I stand and beat –
I stand and beat my heart against the door.


## A Farewell

Remember me and smile, as smiling too,
    I have remembered things that went their way –
    The dolls with which I grew too wise to play –
Or over-wise – and kissed, as children do,

4

And so dismissed them; yes, even as you
   Have done with this poor piece of painted clay –
   Not wantonly, but wisely, shall we say?
As one who, haply, tunes his heart anew.

Only I wish her eyes may not be blue,
   The eyes of the new angel. Ah! she may
Miss something that I found, – perhaps the clue
To those long silences of yours, which grew
   Into one word. And should she not be gay,
   Poor lady! Well, she too must have her day!

## *V.R.I.*

### I
#### *January 22nd, 1901.*

'A Nation's Sorrow.' No. In that strange hour
   We did but note the flagging pulse of day,
   The sudden pause of Time, and turn away
Incredulous of grief; beyond the power
Of question or of tears. Thy people's pain
   Was their perplexity: Thou could'st not be
God's and not England's. Let Thy spirit reign,
   For England is not England without Thee.
Still Thine, Immortal Dead, she still shall stake
   Thy fame against the world, and hold supreme
Thy unsuspended sway. Then lay not down
   Thy sceptre, lest her Empire prove a dream
Of Thine, great, gentle Sleeper, who shalt wake
   When God doth please, to claim another crown.

*II.*
*February 2nd, 1901.*

When, wrapped in the calm majesty of sleep,
    She passes through her people to her rest,
    Has she no smile in slumber? Is her breast,
Even to their sorrow, pulseless? Shall they weep
And She not with them? Nothing is so strange
    As this, that England's passion, be it pain,
    Or joy, or triumph, never shall again
Find voice in her. No change is like this change.

For all this mute indifference of death,
    More dear She is than She has ever been.
    The dark crowd gathers: not 'The Queen! The Queen!'
Upon its lip to-day. A quickened breath –
    She passes – through the hush, the straining gaze,
    The vast, sweet silence of its love and praise.

## To a Little Child in Death

Dear, if little feet make little journeys,
    Thine should not be far;
        Though beyond the faintest star,
        Past earth's last bar,
        Where angels are,
            Thou hast to travel –
Cross the far blue spaces of the sea,
Climb above the tallest tree,
Higher up than many mountains be;
    Sure there is some shorter way for thee,
Since little feet make little journeys.

Then, if smallest limbs are soonest weary,
  Thou should'st soon be there;
    Stumbling up the golden stair,
    Where the angels' shining hair
      Brushes dust from baby faces.
    Very, very gently cling
    To a silver-edged wing,
      And peep from under.
    Then thou'lt see the King,
    Then will many voices sing,
      And thou wilt wonder.
    Wait a little while
    For Him to smile,
      Who calleth thee.
    He who calleth all,
    Both great and small,
    From over mountain, star and sea,
  Doth call the smallest soonest to His knee,
Since smallest limbs are soonest weary.


## At the Convent Gate

'Why do you shrink away, and start and stare? –
  Life frowns to see you leaning at death's gate –
  Not back, but on. Ah! sweet, it is too late –
You cannot cast these kisses from your hair.
Will God's cold breath blow kindly anywhere
  Upon such burning gold? Oh! lips worn white
  With waiting! Love will blossom in a night
And you shall wake to find the roses there!'

'Oh hush! He seems to stir, He lifts His Head.
He smiles. Look where He hangs against the sky.
He never smiled nor stirred, that God of pain
With tired eyes and limbs, above my bed –
But loose me, this is death, I will not die –
Not while He smiles. Oh! Christ, Thine own again!'

## Song

Oh! Sorrow, Sorrow, scarce I knew
    Your name when, shaking down the may
In sport, a little child, I grew
    Afraid to find you at my play.
I heard it ere I looked at you;
    You sang it softly as you came
Bringing your little boughs of yew
    To fling across my gayest game.

Oh! Sorrow, Sorrow, was I fair
    That when I decked me for a bride,
You met me stepping down the stair
    And led me from my lover's side?
Was I so dear you could not spare
    The maid to love, the child to play,
But coming always unaware,
    Must bid and beckon me away?

Oh! Sorrow, Sorrow, is my bed
    So wide and warm that you must lie
Upon it; toss your weary head
    And stir my slumber with your sigh?

I left my love at your behest,
  I waved your little boughs of yew,
But, Sorrow, Sorrow, let me rest,
  For oh! I cannot sleep with you!


## Not for that City

Not for that city of the level sun,
    Its golden streets and glittering gates ablaze –
    The shadeless, sleepless city of white days,
White nights, or nights and days that are as one –
We weary, when all is said, all though, all done,
    We strain our eyes beyond this dusk to see
    What, from the threshold of eternity
We shall step into. No, I think we shun
The splendour of that everlasting glare,
    The clamour of that never-ending song.
    And if for anything we greatly long,
It is for some remote and quiet stair
    Which winds to silence and a space of sleep
    Too sound for waking and for dreams too deep.


## Afternoon Tea

Please you, excuse me, good five-o'clock people,
  I've lost my last hatful of words,
And my heart's in the wood up above the church steeple,
  I'd rather have tea with – the birds.


Gay Kate's stolen kisses, poor Barnaby's scars,
  John's losses and Mary's gains,
Oh! what do they matter, my dears, to the stars
  Or the glow-worms in the lanes!

9

I'd rather lie under the tall elm-trees,
   With old rooks talking loud overhead,
To watch a red squirrel run over my knees,
   Very still on my brackeny bed.

And wonder what feathers the wrens will be taking
   For lining their nests next Spring;
Or why the tossed shadow of boughs in a great wind shaking
   Is such a lovely thing.

## The Little Portress
### (St Gilda de Rhuys)

The stillness of the sunshine lies
   Upon her spirit: silence seems
   To look out from its place of dreams
When suddenly she lifts her eyes
   To waken, for a little space,
   The smile asleep upon her face.

A thousand years of sun and shower,
   The melting of unnumbered snows
   Go to the making of the rose
Which blushes out its little hour.
   So old is Beauty: in its heart
   The ages seem to meet and part.

Like Beauty's self, she holds a clear
   Deep memory of hidden things –
   The music of forgotten springs –
So far she travels back, so near
   She seems to stand to patient truth
   As old as Age, as young as Youth.

That is her window, by the gate,
   Now and again her figure flits
   Across the wall. Long hours she sits
Within: on all who come to wait.
   Her Saviour too is hanging there
   A foot or so above her chair.


'Soeur Marie de l'enfant Jésus,'
   You wrote it in my little book –
   Your shadow-name. Your shadow-look
Is dimmer and diviner too,
   But not to keep: it slips so far
   Beyond us to that golden bar


Where angels, watching from their stair,
   Half-envy you your tranquil days
   Of prayer as exquisite as praise –
Grey twilights softer than their glare
   Of glory: all sweet human things
   Which vanish with the whirr of wings.


Yet will you, when you wing your way
   To whiter worlds, more whitely shine
   Or shed a radiance more divine
Than here you shed from day to day –
   High in His heaven a quiet star,
   Be nearer God than now you are?


## Requiescat

Your birds that call from tree to tree
   Just overhead, and whirl and dart,
Your breeze fresh-blowing from the sea,
   And your sea singing on, Sweetheart.

Your salt scent on the thin, sharp air
    Of this grey dawn's first drowsy hours,
While on the grass shines everywhere
    The yellow starlight of your flowers.

At the road's end your strip of blue
    Beyond that line of naked trees –
Strange that we should remember you
    As if you would remember these!

As if your spirit, swaying yet
    To the old passions, were not free
Of Spring's wild magic, and the fret
    Of the wilder wooing of the sea!

What threat of old imaginings,
    Half-haunted joy, enchanted pain,
Or dread of unfamiliar things
    Should ever trouble you again?

Yet you would wake and want, you said,
    The little whirr of wings, the clear
Gay notes, the wind, the golden bed
    Of the daffodil: and they are here –!

Just overhead, they whirl and dart
    Your birds that call from tree to tree,
Your sea is singing on – Sweetheart,
    Your breeze is flowing from the sea.

Beyond the line of naked trees
    At the road's end, your stretch of blue –
Strange if you should remember these
    As we, ah! God! remember you!

## Péri en Mer
### (Cameret)

One day the friends who stand about my bed
   Will slowly turn from it to speak of me
Indulgently, as of the newly dead,
   Not knowing how I perished by the sea,
That night in summer when the gulls topped white
   The crowded masts cut black against a sky
Of fading rose – where suddenly the light
   Of Youth went out, and I, no longer I,
Climbed home, the homeless ghost I was to be.
   Yet as I passed, they sped me up the heights –
Old seamen round the door of the Abri
   De la Tempête. Even on quiet nights
   So may some ship go down with all her lights
Beyond the sight of watchers on the quay!


## She was a Sinner

Love was my flower, and before He came –
   'Master, there was a garden where it grew
Rank, with the colour of a crimson flame,
   Thy flower too, but knowing not its name
Nor yet that it was Thine, I did not spare
But tore and trampled it and stained my hair,
My hands, my lips, with the red petals; see,
   Drenched with the blood of Thy poor murdered flower
I stood, when suddenly the hour
        Struck for me,

13

And straight I came and wound about Thy Feet
      The strands of shame
Twined with those broken buds: till lo, more sweet,
      More red, yet still the same,
Bright burning blossoms sprang around Thy brow
Beneath the thorns (I saw, I know not how,
The crown which Thou wast afterward to wear
      On that immortal Tree)
And I went out and found my garden very bare,
But swept and watered it, then followed Thee.

There was another garden where to seek
Thee, first, I came in those grey hours
Of the Great Dawn, and knew Thee not till Thou didst speak
My name, that "Mary" like a flash of light
Shot from Thy lips. Thou wast "the gardener" too,
      And then I knew
That evermore our flowers,
Thine, Lord, and mine, shall be a burning white.'

# The Farmer's Bride

(1916)

## The Farmer's Bride

Three Summers since I chose a maid –
Too young maybe – but more's to do
At harvest-time than bide and woo.
    When us was wed she turned afraid
Of love and me and all things human;
Like the shut of a winter's day
Her smile went out, and 'twasn't a woman –
    More like a little frightened fay.
        One night, in the Fall, she runned away.

'Out 'mong the sheep, her be,' they said,
'Should properly have been abed;
But sure enough she wasn't there
Lying awake with her wide brown stare.
So over seven-acre field and up-along across the down
    We chased her, flying like a hare
Before our lanterns. To Church-Town
    All in a shiver and a scare
We caught her, fetched her home at last,
    And turned the key upon her, fast.

She does the work about the house
As well as most, but like a mouse.
    Happy enough to chat and play
    With birds and rabbits and such as they,
    So long as men-folk keep away.
'Not near, not near!' her eyes beseech
When one of us comes within reach.
    The women say that beasts in stall
    Look round like children at her call.
    *I've* hardly heard her speak at all.

Shy as a leveret, swift as he,
Straight and slight as a young larch tree,
Sweet as the first wild violets, she,
To her wild self. But what to me?

The short days shorten, and the oaks are brown,
    The blue smoke rises to the low grey sky,
One leaf in the still air falls slowly down,
    A magpie's spotted feathers lie
On the black earth spread white with rime,
The berries redden up to Christmas-time.
    What's Christmas-time without there be
    Some other in the house than we!

She sleeps up in the attic there
Alone, poor maid. 'Tis but a stair
Betwixt us. Oh! my God! the down,
The soft young down of her, the brown,
The brown of her – her eyes, her hair, her hair!


## Fame

Sometimes in the over-heated house, but not for long,
    Smirking and speaking rather loud,
    I see myself among the crowd,
Where no one fits the singer to his song,
Or sifts the unpainted from the painted faces
Of the people who are always on my stair;
They were not with me when I walked in heavenly places;
                But could I spare
In the blind Earth's great silences and spaces,
    The din, the scuffle, the long stare
    If I went back and it was not there?

Back to the old known things that are the new,
The folded glory of the gorse, the sweet-briar air,
To the larks that cannot praise us, knowing nothing of what we do
    And the divine, wise trees that do not care
Yet, to leave Fame, still with such eyes and that bright hair!
God! If I might! And before I go hence
       Take in her stead
       To our tossed bed,
One little dream, no matter how small, how wild.
Just now, I think I found it in a field, under a fence –
A frail, dead, new-born lamb, ghostly and pitiful and white,
       A blot upon the night,
       The moon's dropped child!


## The Narrow Door

    The narrow door, the narrow door
    On the three steps of which the café children play
    Mostly at shop with pebbles from the shore,
    It is always shut this narrow door
But open for a little while to-day.

And round it, each with pebbles in his hand,
A silenced crowd the café children stand
To see the long box jerking down the bend
Of twisted stair; then set on end,
Quite filling up the narrow door
Till it comes out and does not go in any more.

    Along the quay you see it wind,
The slow black line. Someone pulls up the blind
Of the small window just above the narrow door –

'*Tiens! que veux-tu acheter?*' Renée cries,
  '*Mais, pour quat'sous, des oignons,*' Jean replies
And one pays down with pebbles from the shore.


## The Fête

  To-night again the moon's white mat
  Stretches across the dormitory floor
While outside, like an evil cat
  The *pion* prowls down the dark corridor,
  Planning, I know, to pounce on me in spite
For getting leave to sleep in town last night.
But it was none of us who made that noise.
  Only the old brown owl that hoots and flies
Out of the ivy –; he will say it was us boys –
  *Seigneur mon Dieu!* the *sacré* soul of spies!
  He would like to catch each dream that lies
    Hidden behind our sleepy eyes;
Their dream? but mine –, it is the moon and the wood that sees;
All my long life how I shall hate the trees!

In the *Place d'Armes*, the dusty planes, all Summer through
Dozed with the market women in the sun and scarcely stirred
  To see the quiet things that crossed the square –
A tiny funeral, the flying shadow of a bird,
  The hump-backed barber, Célestin Lemaire,
  Old Madame Michel in her three-wheeled chair,
    And filing past to vespers, two and two,
    The *demoiselles* of the *Pensionnat*
Towed like a ship through the harbour bar
  Safe into port where *le petit Jésus*
Perhaps makes nothing of the look they shot at you –:
  *Si, c'est défendu, mais que voulez-vous?*

It was the sun. The sunshine weaves
A pattern on dull stones: the sunshine leaves
　　The portraiture of dreams upon the eyes
　　　　Before it dies.
　　All Summer through
The dust hung white upon the drowsy planes
Till suddenly they woke with the Autumn rains.


　　It is not only the little boys
　　　Who have hardly got away from toys,
But I, who am seventeen next year
Some nights, in bed, have grown cold to hear
　　　　That lonely passion of the rain
Which makes you think of being dead
And of somewhere living to lay your head
　　　　As if you were a child again
Crying for one thing, known and near
Your empty heart to still the hunger and the fear
　　That pelts and beats with it against the pane.


　　　　But I remember smiling too
At all the sun's soft tricks and those Autumn dreads
　　In Winter time when the grey light broke slowly through
The frosted window-lace to drag us shivering from our beds.
　　And when at dusk the singing wind swung down
Straight from the stars to the dark country roads beyond the
　　　　　　　　　　　　　　　　　　twinkling town,
　　Striking the leafless poplar boughs as he went by
Like some poor stray dog by the wayside lying dead
We left behind us the old world of dread
I and the wind as we strode whistling on under the Winter sky.


And then in Spring for three days came the Fair
　　Just as the planes were starting into bud
Above the caravans: you saw the dancing bear
　　Pass on his chain; and heard the jingle and the thud.

Only four days ago
They let you out of this dull show
To slither down the *montaine russe* and chaff the man *à la tête de
veau*, –
Hit, slick, the bulls eye at the *tir*,
Spin round and round till your head went queer
On the *porcs-roulants*. Oh! là là! la Fête!
*Va pour du vin! et le tête-à-tête*
With the girl who sugars the *gaufres! Pauvrette*
How thin she was; but she smiled, you bet,
As she took your tip – 'One does not forget
The good days, *Monsieur*.' Said with a grace
But *sacrebleu!* what a ghost of a face!
And no fun too for the *demoiselles*
Of the *Pensionnat*, who were hurried past
With their '*Oh, que c'est beau – Ah, qu'elle est belle!*'
A lap-dog's life from first to last!
The good nights are not made for sleep, nor the good days for
dreaming in,
And at the end in the big Circus tent we sat and shook and stewed
like sin!


Some children there had got – but where?
Sent from the South, perhaps – a red bouquet
Of roses sweetening the fetid air
With scent from gardens by some far away blue bay.
They threw one at the dancing bear,
The white clown caught it. From St Rémy's tower
The deep slow bell tolled out the hour.
The black clown, with his dirty grin
Lay, sprawling in the dust as She rode in.


She stood on a white horse –, and suddenly you saw the bend
Of a far-off road at dawn, with Knights riding by –
A field of spears – and then the gallant day
Go out in storm, with ragged clouds low down, sullen and grey

Against red heavens: wild and awful, such a sky
  As witnesses against you at the end
Of a great battle, bugles blowing, blood and dust –
The old *Morte d'Arthur*, fight you must –;
  It died in anger. But it was not death
  That had you by the throat stopping your breath,
She looked like Victory. She rode my way.

She laughed at the black clown and then she flew
     A bird above us on the wing
Of her white arms, and you saw through
A rent in the old tent, a patch of sky
With one dim star. She flew, but not so high –
    And then – she did not fly –,
She stood in the bright moonlight at the door
Of a strange room –, she threw her slippers on the floor –
      Again, again,
    You heard the patter of the rain;
    The starving rain, it was this Thing,
Summer was this, the gold mist in your eyes –;
     Oh! God it dies.
     But after death?
  To-night the splendour and the sting
  Blows backs and catches at your breath,
The smell of beasts, the smell of dust, the scent of all the roses in the
                  world, the sea, the Spring –
The beat of drums, the pad of hoofs, music, the Dream, the Dream,
                  the Enchanted Thing!

At first you scarcely saw her face,
  You knew the maddening feet were there,
What called was that half-hidden, white unrest
To which now and then she pressed
  Her finger tips: but as she slackened pace

And turned and looked at you it grew quite bare:
There was not anything you did not dare: –
Like trumpeters the hours passed until the last day of the Fair.


In the *Place d'Armes* all afternoon
The building birds had sung 'Soon, soon'
The shuttered streets slept sound that night,
It was full moon:
The path into the wood was almost white,
The trees were very still and seemed to stare:
Not far before your soul the Dream flits on,
But when you touch it, it is gone
And quite alone your soul stands there.


Mother of Christ, no one has seen your eyes: how can men pray
Even unto you?
There were only wolves' eyes in the wood –
My Mother is a woman too:
Nothing is true that is not good
With that quick smile of hers, I have heard her say –:
I wish I had gone back home to-day,
I should have watched the light that so gently dies
From our high window, in the Paris skies,
The long straight chain
Of lamps hung out along the Seine:
I would have turned to her and let the rain
Beat on her breast as it does against the pane –:
Nothing will be the same again –;
There is something strange in my little Mother's eyes.
There is something new in the old heavenly air of Spring –
The smell of beasts, the smell of dust –, *The Enchanted Thing!*


All my life long I shall see moonlight on the fern
And the black trunks of trees. Only the hair
Of any woman can belong to God.
The stalks are cruelly broken where we trod,

There had been violets there.
I shall not care
As I used to do when I see the bracken burn.


## Beside the Bed

Someone has shut the shining eyes, straightened and folded
    The wandering hands quietly covering the unquiet breast:
So, smoothed and silenced you lie, like a child, not again to be
                                        questioned or scolded;
    But, for you, not one of us believes that this is rest.

Not so to close the windows down can cloud and deaden
    The blue beyond: or to screen the wavering flame subdue its
                                        breath:
Why, if I lay my cheek to your cheek, your grey lips, like dawn,
                                        would quiver and redden,
    Breaking into the old, odd smile at this fraud of death.

Because all night you have not turned to us or spoken
    It is time for you to wake; your dreams were never very deep:
I, for one, have seen the thin, bright, twisted threads of them
                                        dimmed suddenly and broken,
    This is only a most piteous pretence of sleep!


## In Nunhead Cemetery

It is the clay that makes the earth stick to his spade;
    He fills in holes like this year after year;
The others have gone; they were tired, and half afraid,
    But I would rather be standing here;

There is nowhere else to go. I have seen this place
    From the windows of the train that's going past
Against the sky. This is rain on my face –
    It was raining here when I saw it last.

There is something horrible about a flower;
    This, broken in my hand, is one of those
He threw in just now: it will not live another hour;
    There are thousands more: you do not miss a rose.

One of the children hanging about
    Pointed at the whole dreadful heap and smiled
This morning, after THAT was carried out;
    There is something terrible about a child.

We were like children, last week, in the Strand;
    That was the day you laughed at me
Because I tried to make you understand
    The cheap, stale chap I used to be
    Before I saw the things you made me see.

This is not a real place; perhaps by-and-by
    I shall wake – I am getting drenched with all this rain:
To-morrow I will tell you about the eyes of the Crystal Palace train
    Looking down on us, and you will laugh and I shall see what you
                     see again.

    Not here, not now. We said 'Not yet
    Across our low stone parapet
  Will the quick shadows of the sparrows fall.'

    But still it was a lovely thing
    Through the grey months to wait for Spring
    With the birds that go a-gypsying
  In the parks till the blue seas call.

And next to these you used to care
For the lions in Trafalgar Square,
Who'll stand and speak for London when her bell of Judgment
tolls –
And the gulls at Westminster that were
The old sea-captains' souls.
To-day again the brown tide splashes, step by step, the river stair,
And the gulls are there!

By a month we have missed our Day:
The children would have hung about
Round the carriage and over the way
As you and I came out.

We should have stood on the gulls' black cliffs and heard the sea
And seen the moon's white track,
I would have called, you would have come to me
And kissed me back.

You have never done that: I do not know
Why I stood staring at your bed
And heard you, though you spoke so low,
But could not reach your hands, your little head.
There was nothing we could not do, you said,
And you went, and I let you go!

Now I will burn you back, I will burn you through,
Though I am damned for it we two will lie
And burn, here where the starlings fly
To these white stones from the wet sky –;
Dear, you will say this is not I –
It would not be you, it would not be you!

If for only a little while
You will think of it you will understand,
If you will touch my sleeve and smile
As you did that morning in the Strand

         I can wait quietly with you
         Or go away if you want me to –
God! What is God? but your face has gone and your hand!
         Let me stay here too.

         When I was quite a little lad
       At Christmas time we went half mad
         For joy of all the toys we had,
And then we used to sing about the sheep
         The shepherds watched by night;
We used to pray to Christ to keep
         Our small souls safe till morning light –
I am scared, I am staying with you to-night –
                Put me to sleep.

I shall stay here: here you can see the sky;
The houses in the streets are much too high;
         There is no one left to speak to there;
         Here they are everywhere,
And just above them fields and fields of roses lie –
If he would dig it all up again they would not die.

## The Pedlar

Lend me a little while the key
    That locks your heavy heart, and I'll give you back –
Rarer than books and ribbons and beads bright to see –
    This little Key of Dreams out of my pack.

The road, the road, beyond men's bolted doors,
    There shall I walk and you go free of me,
For yours lies North across the moors
    And mine South. To what sea?

How if we stopped and let our solemn selves go by,
    While my gay ghost caught and kissed yours, as ghosts don't do,
And by the wayside this forgotten you and I
    Sat, and were twenty-two?

Give me the key that locks your tired eyes,
    And I will lend you this one from my pack,
Brighter than coloured beads and painted books that make men wise:
    Take it. No, give it back!


## *Pécheresse*

Down the long quay the slow boats glide,
    While here and there a house looms white
Against the gloom of the waterside,
    And some high window throws a light
    As they sail out into the night.

At dawn they will bring in again
    To women knitting on the quay
Who wait for him, their man of men;
    I stand with them, and watch the sea
    Which may have taken mine from me.

Just so the long days come and go.
    The nights, ma Doué! the nights are cold!
Our Lady's heart is as frozen snow,
    Since this one sin I have not told;
    And I shall die or perhaps grow old

Before he comes. The foreign ships
   Bring many a one of face and name
As strange as his, to buy your lips,
   A gold piece for a scarlet shame
   Like mine. But mine was not the same.

One night was ours, one short grey day
   Of sudden sin, unshrived, untold.
He found me, and I lost the way
   To Paradise for him. I sold
   My soul for love and not for gold.

He bought my soul, but even so,
   My face is all that he has seen,
His is the only face I know,
And in the dark church, like a screen,
   It shuts God out; it comes between.

While in some narrow foreign street
   Or loitering on the crowded quay,
Who knows what others he may meet
   To turn his eyes away from me?
   Many are fair to such as he!

There is but one for such as I
   To love, to hate, to hunger for.
I shall, perhaps, grow old and die,
   With one short day to spend and store,
   One night, in all my life, no more.

Just so the long days come and go,
   Yet this one sin I will not tell
Though Mary's heart is as frozen snow
And all nights are cold for one warmed too well.
   But, oh! ma Doué! *the nights of Hell!*

## The Changeling

Toll no bell for me, dear Father, dear Mother,
                Waste no sighs.
There are my sisters, there is my little brother
  Who plays in the place called Paradise,
Your children all, your children for ever,
                But I, so wild,
Your disgrace, with the queer brown face, was never,
  Never, I know, but half your child!

In the garden at play, all day, last summer,
                Far and away I heard
The sweet 'tweet-tweet' of a strange new-comer,
  The dearest, clearest call of a bird.
It lived down there in the deep green hollow,
  My own old home, and the fairies say
The word of a bird is a thing to follow,
  So I was away a night and a day.

One evening too, by the nursery fire,
  We snuggled close and sat round so still,
When suddenly as the wind blew higher,
  Something scratched on the window-sill.
A pinched brown face peered in, I shivered;
  No one listened or seemed to see;
The arms of it waved and the wings of it quivered,
  Whoo – I knew it had come for me!
  Some are as bad as bad can be!
All night long they danced in the rain,
  Round and round in a dripping chain,
Threw their caps at the window-pane,

Tried to make me scream and shout
And fling the bedclothes all about:
    I meant to stay in bed that night,
And if only you had left a light
    They would never have got me out!


Sometimes I wouldn't speak, you see,
    Or answer when you spoke to me,
Because in the long still dusks of Spring
You can hear the whole world whispering:
    The shy green grasses making love,
    The feathers grow on the dear, grey dove,
    The tiny heart of the redstart beat,
    The patter of the squirrel's feet,
The pebbles pushing in the silver streams,
The rushes talking in their dreams,
    The swish-swish of the bat's black wings,
    The wild-wood bluebell's sweet ting-tings,
        Humming and hammering at your ear,
        Everything there is to hear
In the heart of hidden things.
    But not in the midst of the nursery riot,
    That's why I wanted to be quiet,
        Couldn't do my sums, or sing,
        Or settle down to anything.
And when, for that, I was sent upstairs
    I *did* kneel down to say my prayers;
But the King who sits on your high church steeple
    Has nothing to do with us fairy people!


Times I pleased you, dear Father, dear Mother,
    Learned all my lessons and liked to play,
And dearly I loved the little pale brother
    Whom some other bird must have called away.

Why did They bring me here to make me
   Not quite bad and not quite good,
Why unless They're wicked, do They want, in spite to take me
    Back to Their wet, wild wood?
Now, every night I shall see the windows shining,
   The gold lamp's glow, and the fire's red gleam,
While the best of us are twining twigs and the rest of us are whining
    In the hollow by the stream.
Black and chill are Their nights on the wold;
   And They live so long and They feel no pain:
I shall grow up, but never grow old,
   I shall always, always be very cold,
    I shall never come back again!


## Ken


The town is old and very steep,
   A place of bells and cloisters and grey towers,
And black-clad people walking in their sleep –
   A nun, a priest, a woman taking flowers
   To her new grave; and watched from end to end
   By the great Church above, through the still hours
    But in the morning and the early dark
The children wake to dart from doors and call
Down the wide, crooked street, where, at the bend,
    Before it climbs up to the park,
Ken's is the gabled house facing the Castle wall.

When first I came upon him there
Suddenly, on the half-lit stair,
I think I hardly found a trace
Of likeness to a human face

    In his. And I said then
If in His image God made men,
Some other must have made poor Ken –
But for his eyes which looked at you
As two red, wounded stars might do.

He scarcely spoke, you scarcely heard,
    His voice broke off in little jars
To tears sometimes. An uncouth bird
    He seemed as he ploughed up the street,
Groping, with knarred, high-lifted feet
    And arms thrust out as if to beat
        Always against a threat of bars.

    And oftener than not there'd be
    A child just higher than his knee
Trotting beside him. Through his dim
    Long twilight this, at least, shone clear,
    That all the children and the deer,
        Whom every day he went to see
Out in the park, belonged to him.

    'God help the folk that next him sits
    He fidgets so, with his poor wits.'
The neighbours said on Sunday nights
When he would go to Church to 'see the lights!'
    Although for these he used to fix
    His eyes upon a crucifix
    In a dark corner, staring on
    Till everybody else had gone.
    And sometimes, in his evil fits,
You could not move him from his chair –
You did not look at him as he sat there,
    Biting his rosary to bits.
While pointing to the Christ he tried to say
        'Take it away.'

Nothing was dead:
He said 'a bird' if he picked up a broken wing,
    A perished leaf or any such thing
        Was just 'a rose'; and once when I had said
    He must not stand and knock there any more,
    He left a twig on the mat outside my door.


    Not long ago
The last thrush stiffened in the snow,
    While black against a sullen sky
        The sighing pines stood by.
But now the wind has left our rattled pane
To flutter the hedge-sparrow's wing,
The birches in the wood are red again
        And only yesterday
The larks went up a little way to sing
        What lovers say
    Who loiter in the lanes to-day;
    The buds begin to talk of May
    With learned rooks on city trees,
        And if God please
        With all of these
We too, shall see another Spring.


But in that red brick barn upon the hill
    I wonder – can one own the deer,
And does one walk with children still
        As one did here –


    Do roses grow
Beneath those twenty windows in a row –
        And if some night
When you have not seen any light
They cannot move you from your chair
        What happens there?
        I do not know.

So when they took
Ken to that place, I did not look
    After he called and turned on me
    His eyes. These I shall see –


## A Quoi Bon Dire?


Seventeen years ago you said
Something that sounded like Good-bye;
    And everybody thinks that you are dead,
                        But I.


So I, as I grow stiff and cold
To this and that say Good-bye too;
    And everybody sees that I am old
                        But you.


And one fine morning in a sunny lane
Some boy and girl will meet and kiss and swear
    That nobody can love their way again
                        While over there
You will have smiled, I shall have tossed your hair.


## The Quiet House


When we were children old Nurse used to say,
    The house was like an auction or a fair
    Until the lot of us were safe in bed.
    It has been quiet as the country-side
    Since Ted and Janey and then Mother died

And Tom crossed Father and was sent away.
After the lawsuit he could not hold up his head,
    Poor Father, and he does not care
    For people here, or to go anywhere.

To get away to Aunt's for that week-end
    Was hard enough; (since then, a year ago,
    He scarcely lets me slip out of his sight –)
At first I did not like my cousin's friend,
    I did not think I should remember him:
    His voice has gone, his face is growing dim
And if I like him now I do not know.
    He frightened me before he smiled –
    He did not ask me if he might –
    He said that he would come one Sunday night,
    He spoke to me as if I were a child.

No year has been like this that has just gone by;
    It may be that what Father says is true,
If things are so it does not matter why:
    But everything has burned, and not quite through.
    The colours of the world have turned
    To flame, the blue, the gold has burned
In what used to be such a leaden sky.
When you are burned quite through you die.

    Red is the strangest pain to bear;
In Spring the leaves on the budding trees;
In Summer the roses are worse than these,
    More terrible than they are sweet:
    A rose can stab you across the street
        Deeper than any knife:
    And the crimson haunts you everywhere –
Thin shafts of sunlight, like the ghosts of reddened swords have
                                                        struck our stair
As if, coming down, you had spilt your life.

I think that my soul is red
Like the soul of a sword or a scarlet flower:
    But when these are dead
    They have had their hour.

    I shall have had mine, too,
      For from head to feet,
I am burned and stabbed half through,
      And the pain is deadly sweet.

    The things that kill us seem
      Blind to the death they give:
    It is only in our dream
      The things that kill us live.

The room is shut where Mother died,
    The other rooms are as they were,
The world goes on the same outside,
    The sparrows fly across the Square,
    The children play as we four did there,
    The trees grow green and brown and bare,
The sun shines on the dead Church spire,
    And nothing lives here but the fire,
While Father watches from his chair
          Day follows day
The same, or now and then, a different grey,
          Till, like his hair,
Which Mother said was wavy once and bright,
          They will all turn white.

 · To-night I heard a bell again –
Outside it was the same mist of fine rain,
The lamps just lighted down the long, dim street,
          No one for me –
    I think it is myself I go to meet:
I do not care; some day I *shall* not think; I shall not *be*!

## On the Asylum Road

Theirs is the house whose windows – every pane –
   Are made of darkly stained or clouded glass:
Sometimes you come upon them in the lane,
   The saddest crowd that you will ever pass.

But still we merry town or village folk
   Throw to their scattered stare a kindly grin,
And think no shame to stop and crack a joke
   With the incarnate wages of man's sin.

None but ourselves in our long gallery we meet,
   The moor-hen stepping from her reeds with dainty feet,
     The hare-bell bowing on his stem,
Dance not with us; their pulses beat
   To fainter music; nor do we to them
      Make their life sweet.

The gayest crowd that they will ever pass
   Are we to brother-shadows in the lane:
Our windows, too, are clouded glass
   To them, yes, every pane!

## Jour des Morts
### (Cimetière Montparnasse)

Sweetheart, is this the last of all our posies
   And little festivals, my flowers are they
But white and wistful ghosts of gayer roses
   Shut with you in this grim garden? Not to-day,
Ah! no! come out with me before the grey gate closes
   It is your fête and here is your bouquet!

## The Forest Road

The forest road,
The infinite straight road stretching away
World without end: the breathless road between the walls
Of the black listening trees: the hushed, grey road
Beyond the window that you shut to-night
Crying that you would look at it by day –
There is a shadow there that sings and calls,
But not for you. Oh! hidden eyes that plead in sleep
Against the lonely dark, if I could touch the fear
And leave it kissed away on quiet lids –
If I could hush these hands that are half-awake
Groping for me in sleep I could go free.
I wish that God would take them out of mine
And fold them like the wings of frightened birds
Shot cruelly down, but fluttering into quietness so soon,
Broken, forgotten things. There is no grief for them in the green
Spring
When the new birds fly back to the old trees.
But it shall not be so with you. I will look back; I wish I knew that
God would stand
Smiling and looking down on you when morning comes
To hold you, when you wake, closer than I
So gently though: and not with famished lips or hungry arms:
He does not hurt the frailest, dearest things
As we do in the dark. See, dear, your hair –
I must unloose this hair that sleeps and dreams
About my face and clings like the brown weed
To drowned, delivered things, tossed by the tired sea
Back to the beaches. Oh! your hair! If you had lain
A long time dead on the rough, glistening ledge
Of some black cliff, forgotten by the tide,
The raving winds would tear, the dripping brine would rust away
Fold after fold of all the loveliness

That wraps you round and makes you, lying here,
The passionate fragrance that the roses are.
But death would spare the glory of your head
In the long sweetness of the hair that does not die:
The spray would leap to it in every storm,
The scent of the unsilenced sea would linger on
In these dark waves and round the Silence that was you –
Only the nesting gulls would hear – but there would still be whispers
                                                    in your hair.
Keep them for me. Keep them for me. What *is* this singing on the
                                                    road
That makes all other music like the music in a dream –
Dumb to the dancing and the marching feet. You know, in dreams,
                                                    you see
Old pipers playing that you cannot hear
And ghostly drums that only seem to beat. This seems to climb:
Is it the music of a larger place? It makes our room too small: it is like
                                                    a stair,
A calling stair that climbs up to a smile you scarcely see,
Dim but so waited for; and *you* know what a smile is, how it calls,
How if I smiled you always ran to me.
Now you must sleep forgetfully, as children do.
There is a Spirit sits by us in sleep
Nearer than those who walk with us in the bright day.
I think he has a tranquil, saving face: I think he came
Straight from the hills: he may have suffered there in time gone by,
And once, from those forsaken heights, looked down,
Lonely himself, on all the lonely sorrows of the earth.
It is his kingdom – Sleep. If I could leave you there –
If without waking you I could get up and reach the door –
We used to go together. – Shut, scared eyes,
Poor, desolate, desperate hands, it is not I
Who thrust you off. No, take your hands away –
I cannot strike your lonely hands. Yes, I have struck your heart,
It did not come so near. Then lie you there
Dear and wild heart behind this quivering snow

With two red stains on it: and I will strike and tear
Mine out, and scatter it to yours. Oh! throbbing dust,
You that were life, our little wind-blown hearts!
                    The road! the road!
There is a shadow there: I see my soul,
I hear my soul, singing among the trees!


## Madeleine in Church

Here, in the darkness, where this plaster saint
        Stands nearer than God stands to our distress,
And one small candle shines, but not so faint
        As the far lights of everlastingness
I'd rather kneel than over there, in open day
        Where Christ is hanging, rather pray
            To something more like my own clay,
                    Not too divine;
            For, once, perhaps my little saint
            Before he got his niche and crown,
        Had one short stroll about the town;
        It brings him closer, just that taint
                And anyone can wash the paint
        Off our poor faces, his and mine!

Is that why I see Monty now? equal to any saint, poor boy, as good as
                                                        gold,
But still, with just the proper trace
Of earthliness on his shining wedding face;
And then gone suddenly blank and old
The hateful day of the divorce:
Stuart got his, hands down, of course
Crowing like twenty cocks and grinning like a horse:
But Monty took it hard. All said and done I liked him best, –
He was the first, he stands out clearer than the rest.

It seems too funny all we other rips
Should have immortal souls; Monty and Redge quite damnably
Keep theirs afloat while we go down like scuttled ships. –
It's funny too, how easily we sink,
One might put up a monument, I think
To half the world and cut across it 'Lost at Sea!'
I should drown Jim, poor little sparrow, if I netted him to-night –
No, it's no use this penny light –
Or my poor saint with his tin-pot crown –
The trees of Calvary are where they were,
When we are sure that we can spare
The tallest, let us go and strike it down
And leave the other two still standing there.
I, too, would ask Him to remember me
If there were any Paradise beyond this earth that I could see.


Oh! quiet Christ who never knew
The poisonous fangs that bite us through
And make us do the things we do,
See how we suffer and fight and die,
How helpless and how low we lie,
God holds You, and You hang so high,
Though no one looking long at You,
Can think You do not suffer too,
But, up there, from your still, star-lighted tree
What can You know, what can You really see
Of this dark ditch, the soul of me!


We are what we are: when I was half a child I could not sit
Watching black shadows on green lawns and red carnations burning
in the sun,
Without paying so heavily for it
That joy and pain, like any mother and her unborn child were
almost one.
I could hardly bear

43

The dreams upon the eyes of white geraniums in the
dusk,
The thick, close voice of musk,
The jessamine music on the thin night air,
Or, sometimes, my own hands about me anywhere –
The sight of my own face (for it was lovely then) even the scent of
my own hair,
Oh! there was nothing, nothing that did not sweep to the
high seat
Of laughing gods, and then blow down and beat
My soul into the highway dust, as hoofs do the dropped roses of the
street.
I think my body was my soul,
And when we are made thus
Who shall control
Our hands, our eyes, the wandering passion of our feet,
Who shall teach us
To thrust the world out of our heart; to say, till perhaps in death,
When the race is run
And it is forced from us with our last breath
'Thy will be done'?
If it is Your will that we should be content with the tame, bloodless
things,
As pale as angels smirking by, with folded wings.
Oh! I know Virtue, and the peace it brings!
The temperate, well-worn smile
The one man gives you, when you are evermore his own:
And afterwards the child's, for a little while,
With its unknowing and all-seeing eyes
So soon to change, and make you feel how quick
The clock goes round. If one had learned the trick –
(How does one though?) quite early on,
Of long green pastures under placid skies,
One might be walking now with patient truth.
What did we ever care for it, who have asked for youth,
When, oh! my God! this is going or has gone?

There is a portrait of my mother, at nineteen,
  With the black spaniel, standing by the garden seat,
  The dainty head held high against the painted green
And throwing out the youngest smile, shy, but half haughty and half
                                                            sweet.

  Her picture then: but simply Youth, or simply Spring
            To me to-day: a radiance on the wall,
            So exquisite, so heart-breaking a thing
      Beside the mask that I remember, shrunk and small,
            Sapless and lined like a dead leaf,
All that was left of oh! the loveliest face, by time and grief!


  And in the glass, last night, I saw a ghost behind my chair –
  Yet why remember it, when one can still go moderately gay –?
      Or could – with any one of the old crew,
            But oh! these boys! the solemn way
      They take you, and the things they say –
      This 'I have only as long as you'
  When you remind them you are not precisely twenty-two –
      Although at heart perhaps – God! if it were
            Only the face, only the hair!
      If Jim had written to me as he did to-day
      A year ago – and now it leaves me cold –
            I know what this means, old, old, *old!*
      *Et avec ça – mais on a vécu, tout se paie.*


That is not always true: there was my Mother – (well at least the dead
                                                            are free!)
  Yoked to the man that Father was; yoked to the woman I am,
                                                            Monty too;
  The little portress at the Convent School, stewing in hell so
                                                            patiently;
The poor, fair boy who shot himself at Aix. And what of me – and
                                                            what of me?
  But I, I paid for what I had, and they for nothing. No, one cannot
                                                            see

How it shall be made up to them in some serene eternity.
If there were fifty heavens God could not give us back the child who
went or never came;
Here, on our little patch of this great earth, the sun of any
darkened day,
Not one of all the starry buds hung on the hawthorn trees of last
year's May,
No shadow from the sloping fields of yesterday;
For every hour they slant across the hedge a different way,
The shadows are never the same.

'Find rest in Him' One knows the parsons' tags –
Back to the fold, across the evening fields, like any flock of
baa-ing sheep:
Yes, it may be, when He has shorn, led us to slaughter, torn the
bleating soul in us to rags,
For so He giveth His belovèd sleep.
Oh! He will take us stripped and done,
Driven into His heart. So we are won:
Then safe, safe are we? in the shelter of His everlasting
wings –
I do not envy Him his victories, His arms are full of broken
things.

But I shall not be in them. Let him take
The finer ones, the easier to break.
And they are not gone, yet, for me, the lights, the colours, the
perfumes,
Though now they speak rather in sumptuous rooms,
In silks and in gem-like wines;
Here, even, in this corner where my little candle shines
And overhead the lancet-window glows
With golds and crimsons you could almost drink
To know how jewels taste, just as I used to think
There was the scent in every red and yellow rose
Of all the sunsets. But this place is grey,

And much too quiet. No one here,
Why, this is awful, this is fear!
Nothing to see, no face,
Nothing to hear except your heart beating in space
As if the world was ended. Dead at last!
Dead soul, dead body, tied together fast.
These to go on with and alone, to the slow end:
No one to sit with, really, or to speak to, friend to friend:
Out of the long procession, black or white or red
Not one left now to say 'Still I am here, then see you, dear, lay here
your head.'

Only the doll's house looking on the Park
To-night, all nights, I know, when the man puts the lights out,
very dark.
With, upstairs, in the blue and gold box of a room, just the maids'
footsteps overhead,
Then utter silence and the empty world – the room – the bed –
The corpse! No, not quite dead, while this cries out in
me,
But nearly: very soon to be
A handful of forgotten dust –
There must be someone. Christ! there must,
Tell me there *will* be some one. Who?
If there were no one else, could it be You?

How old was Mary out of whom you cast
So many devils? Was she young or perhaps for years
She had sat staring, with dry eyes, at this and that man going past
Till suddenly she saw You on the steps of Simon's house
And stood and looked at you through tears.
I think she must have known by those
The thing, for what it was that had come to her.
For some of us there is a passion, I suppose
So far from earthly cares and earthly fears

That in its stillness you can hardly stir
　　　　Or in its nearness, lift your hand,
So great that you have simply got to stand
Looking at it through tears, through tears.
Then straight from these there broke the kiss,
　　　　I think You must have known by this
The thing, for what it was, that had come to You:
　　　　She did not love You like the rest,
It was in her own way, but at the worst, the best,
　　　　She gave you something altogether new.
　　　　And through it all, from her, no word,
　　　　She scarcely saw You, scarcely heard:
Surely You knew when she so touched You with her
　　　　　　　　　　　　　　hair,
　　　　Or by the wet cheek lying there,
And while her perfume clung to You from head to feet all through
　　　　　　　　　　　　　　the day
　　　　That You can change the things for which we care,
　　　　But even You, unless You kill us, not the way.

　　　　This, then was peace for her, but passion too.
　　　　I wonder was it like a kiss that once I knew,
　　　　The only one that I would care to take
Into the grave with me, to which if there were afterwards, to wake.
　　　　Almost as happy as the carven dead
　　　　In some dim chancel lying head by head
We slept with it, but face to face, the whole night through –
One breath, one throbbing quietness, as if the thing behind our lips
　　　　　　　　　　　　　　was endless life,
Lost, as I woke, to hear in the strange earthly dawn, his 'Are you
　　　　　　　　　　　　　　there?'
　　　　And lie still, listening to the wind outside, among the
　　　　　　　　　　　　　　firs.

So Mary chose the dream of Him for what was left to her of night
and day,
It is the only truth: it is the dream in us that neither life nor death nor
any other thing can take away:
But if she had not touched Him in the doorway of the dream could
she have cared so much?
She was a sinner, we are what we are: the spirit afterwards, but
first, the touch.

And He has never shared with me my haunted house beneath the
trees
Of Eden and Calvary, with its ghosts that have not any eyes for tears,
And the happier guests who would not see, or if they did, remember
these,
Though they lived there a thousand years.
Outside, too gravely looking at me, He seems to stand,
And looking at Him, if my forgotten spirit came
Unwillingly back, what could it claim
Of those calm eyes, that quiet speech,
Breaking like a slow tide upon the beach,
The scarred, not quite human hand? –
Unwillingly back to the burden of old imaginings
When it has learned so long not to think, not to be,
Again, again it would speak as it has spoken to me of things
That I shall not see!

I cannot bear to look at this divinely bent and gracious head:
When I was small I never quite believed that He was dead:
And at the Convent school I used to lie awake in bed
Thinking about His hands. It did not matter what they said,
He was alive to me, so hurt, so hurt! And most of all in Holy Week
When there was no one else to see
I used to think it would not hurt me too, so terribly,
If He had ever seemed to notice me
Or, if, for once, He would only speak.

## *Exspecto Resurrectionem*

Oh! King who hast the key
    Of that dark room,
The last which prisons us but held not Thee,
    Thou know'st its gloom.
Dost Thou a little love this one
    Shut in to-night,
Young and so piteously alone,
    Cold – out of sight?
Thou know'st how hard and bare
The pillow of that new-made narrow bed,
    Then leave not there
    So dear a head!

Poems added in the second edition of
## *The Farmer's Bride*
(1921)

## On the Road to the Sea

We passed each other, turned and stopped for half an hour, then
                                                              went our way,
    I who make other women smile did not make you –
But no man can move mountains in a day.
    So this hard thing is yet to do.

But first I want your life: – before I die I want to see
    The world that lies behind the strangeness of your eyes,
There is nothing gay or green there for my gathering, it may be,
    Yet on brown fields there lies
A haunting purple bloom: is there not something in grey skies
    And in grey sea?
    I want what world there is behind your eyes,
    I want your life and you will not give it me.

    Now, if I look, I see you walking down the years,
    Young, and through August fields – a face, a thought, a swinging
                                                              dream perched on a stile –;
    I would have liked (so vile we are!) to have taught you tears
    But most to have made you smile.

    To-day is not enough or yesterday: God sees it all –
Your length on sunny lawns, the wakeful rainy nights –; tell me –;
    (how vain to ask), but it is not a question – just a call –;
Show me then, only your notched inches climbing up the garden
                                                              wall,
    I like you best when you are small.

    Is this a stupid thing to say
    Not having spent with you one day?
No matter; I shall never touch your hair
Or hear the little tick behind your breast,
    Still it is there,

And as a flying bird
Brushes the branches where it may not rest
I have brushed your hand and heard
The child in you: I like that best.

So small, so dark, so sweet; and were you also then too grave and
wise?
Always I think. Then put your far off little hand in mine; – Oh!
let it rest;
I will not stare into the early world beyond the opening eyes,
Or vex or scare what I love best.

But I want your life before mine bleeds away –
Here – not in heavenly hereafters – soon, –
I want your smile this very afternoon,
(The last of all my vices, pleasant people used to say,
I wanted and I sometimes got – the Moon!)

You know, at dusk, the last bird's cry,
And round the house the flap of the bat's low flight,
Trees that go black against the sky
And then – how soon the night!

No shadow of you on any bright road again,
And at the darkening end of this – what voice? whose kiss? As if you'd
say!
It is not I who have walked with you, it will not be I who take
away
Peace, peace, my little handful of the gleaner's grain
From your reaped fields at the shut of day.

Peace! Would you not rather die
Reeling, – with all the cannons at your ear?
So, at least, would I,
And I may not be here

To-night, to-morrow morning or next year.
Still, I will let you keep your life a little while,
      See dear?
    *I have made you smile.*


## The Sunlit House

White through the gate it gleamed and slept
    In shuttered sunshine: the parched garden flowers
Their fallen petals from the beds unswept,
    Like children unloved and ill-kept
      Dreamed through the hours.
Two blue hydrangeas by the blistered door, burned brown,
    Watched there and no one in the town
    Cared to go past it, night or day,
    Though why this was they wouldn't say.
But, I the stranger, knew that I must stay,
    Pace up the weed-grown paths and down,
    Till one afternoon – there is just a doubt –
    But I fancy I heard a tiny shout –
    From an upper window a bird flew out –
      And I went my way.


## The Shade-Catchers

I think they were about as high
As haycocks are. They went running by
Catching bits of shade in the sunny street:
'I've got one,' cried sister to brother.
    'I've got two.' 'Now I've got another.'
But scudding away on their little bare feet,
They left the shade in the sunny street.

## Le Sacré-Coeur
(Montmartre)

It is dark up here on the heights,
    Between the dome and the stars it is quiet too,
While down there under the crowded lights
    Flares the importunate face of you,
Dear Paris of the hot white hands, the scarlet lips, the scented hair,
        *Une jolie fille à vendre, très cher*;
        A thing of gaiety, a thing of sorrow,
        Bought to-night, possessed, and tossed
        Back to the mart again to-morrow,
            Worth and over, what you cost;
While half your charm is that you are
Withal, like some unpurchasable star,
    So old, so young and infinite and lost.

It is dark on the dome-capped hill,
    Serenely dark, divinely still,
Yet here is the Man who bought you first
    Dying of his immortal smart,
Your Lover, the King with the broken heart,
        Who while you, feasting, drink your fill,
            Pass round the cup
            Not looking up,
Calls down to you, 'I thirst.'

'A king with a broken heart! *Mon Dieu!*
    One breaks so many, *cela peut se croire*,
To remember all *c'est la mer à boire*,
    And the first, *mais comme c'est vieux*.
Perhaps there is still some keepsake – or
    One has possibly sold it for a song:
*On ne peut pas toujours pleurer les morts*,
    And this One – He has been dead so long!'

## Song

Love Love to-day, my dear
Love is not always here
Wise maids know how soon grows sere
    The greenest leaf of Spring.
      But no man knoweth
      Whither it goeth
      When the wind bloweth
        So frail a thing.

Love Love, my dear, to-day
If the ship's in the bay
If the bird has come your way
    That sings on summer trees.
      When his song faileth
      And the ship saileth
      No voice availeth
        To call back these.

## Saturday Market

Bury your heart in some deep green hollow
    Or hide it up in a kind old tree
Better still, give it the swallow
    When she goes over the sea.

In Saturday Market there's eggs a 'plenty
    And dead-alive ducks with their legs tied down –
Grey old gaffers and boys of twenty –
    Girls and the women of the town –

Pitchers and sugar-sticks, ribbons and laces
    Posies and whips and dicky-birds' seed,
Silver pieces and smiling faces,
    In Saturday Market they've all they need.

What were you showing in Saturday Market
    That set it grinning from end to end
Girls and gaffers and boys of twenty –?
    Cover it close with your shawl, my friend –
Hasten you home with the laugh behind you,
    Over the down – out of sight,
Fasten your door, though no one will find you,
    No one will look on a Market night.

See you, the shawl is wet, take out from under
    The red, dead thing. In the white of the moon
On the flags does it stir again? Well, and no wonder –
    Best make an end of it, bury it soon.
If there is blood on the hearth who'll know it?
    Or blood on the stairs,
When a murder is over and done why show it?
    In Saturday Market nobody cares.

Then lie you straight on your bed for a short short weeping,
    And still for a long, long rest,
There's never a one in the town so sure of sleeping
    As you, in the house on the down, with a hole in your breast.

    Think no more of the swallow,
        Forget you, the sea,
    Never again remember the deep green hollow,
        Or the top of the kind old tree!

## Arracombe Wood

Some said, because he wud'n spaik
Any words to women but Yes and No,
Nor put out his hand for Parson to shake
He mun be bird-witted. But I do go
By the lie of the barley that he did sow,
And I wish no better thing than to hold a rake
Like Dave, in his time, or to see him mow.

Put up in churchyard a month ago,
'A bitter old soul,' they said, but it wadn't so.
His heart were in Arracombe Wood where he'd used to go
To sit and talk wi' his shadder till sun went low,
Though what it was all about us'll never know.
And there baint no mem'ry in the place
Of th' old man's footmark, nor his face;
Arracombe Wood do think more of a crow –
'Will be violets there in the Spring: in Summer time the spider's lace;
And come the Fall, the whizzle and race
Of the dry, dead leaves when the wind gies chase;
And on the Eve of Christmas, fallin' snow.

## Sea Love

Tide be runnin' the great world over;
T'was only last June-month, I mind, that we
Was thinkin' the toss and the call in the breast of the lover
So everlastin' as the sea.

Heer's the same little fishes that sputter and swim
    Wi' the moon's old glim on the grey, wet sand
An' him no more to me nor me to him
    Than the wind goin' over my hand.


## The Road to Kérity

Do you remember the two old people we passed on the road to
                              Kérity,
Resting their sack, on the stones, by the drenched wayside,
Looking at us with their lightless eyes through the driving rain and
                           then out again
To the rocks and the long white line of the tide:
Frozen ghosts that were children once, husband and wife, father and
                             mother,
Looking at us with those frozen eyes –; have you ever seen anything
                      quite so chilled or so old?
      But we – with our arms about each other,
           We did not feel the cold!


## I Have Been Through the Gates

His heart, to me, was a place of palaces and pinnacles and shining
                         towers;
I saw it then as we see things in dreams –; I do not remember how
                      long I slept;
I remember the trees and the high, white walls, and how the sun was
                      always on the towers;
The walls are standing to-day, and the gates: I have been through the
                  gates, I have groped, I have crept

Back, back –. There is dust in the streets and blood; they are empty;
darkness is over them;
His heart is a place with the lights gone out, forsaken by great winds
and the heavenly rain, unclean and unswept,
Like the heart of the holy city, old, blind, beautiful Jerusalem,
Over which Christ wept.

## The Cenotaph

Not yet will those measureless fields be green again
Where only yesterday the wild sweet blood of wonderful youth was
shed;
There is a grave whose earth must hold too long, too deep a stain,
Though for ever over it we may speak as proudly as we may tread.
But here, where the watchers by lonely hearths from the thrust of an
inward sword have more slowly bled,
We shall build the Cenotaph: Victory, winged, with Peace, winged
too, at the column's head.
And over the stairway, at the foot – oh! here, leave desolate,
passionate hands to spread
Violets, roses, and laurel, with the small sweet twinkling country
things
Speaking so wistfully of other Springs
From the little gardens of little places where son or sweetheart was
born and bred.
In splendid sleep, with a thousand brothers
To lovers – to mothers
Here, too, lies he:
Under the purple, the green, the red,
It is all young life: it must break some women's hearts to see
Such a brave, gay coverlet to such a bed!
Only, when all is done and said,
God is not mocked and neither are the dead.

For this will stand in our Market-place –
               Who'll sell, who'll buy
              (Will you or I
Lie each to each with the better grace)?
While looking into every busy whore's and huckster's face
As they drive their bargains, is the Face
Of God: and some young, piteous, murdered face.

*The Wheat*

## *The Wheat*

'DON'T LET them cut the Wheat' he had said, sitting up in bed and falling back on it, his face towards the window opening on to the row of windows opposite, in the brickwork of the London street. All through his illness there had been no delirium so that this touch of it at the end seemed strange to them. 'Up to that moment he was quite himself and they were so unlike him' Amy said to her Mother repeating his words about the cutting of the wheat.

No one had known, and half the time he had hardly known himself, but lying there, taking medicines and being read to, he saw how, on and off, it had been with him ever since he was a boy, that Something behind him which he hadn't got at and that other sense of not being altogether Here.

Work took it off and he was always at it, in or out of the house, but even at the Bank, taking in cheques and handing out gold across the counter, now and then it came to him that it wasn't he who was doing it; that he was really somewhere else and that the cheques and the scales and the sovereigns were not real things. He hadn't much, but all the same he hated money, – the look, the feel, the idea of it, perhaps because he stood in a bath of it (someone else's bath) all day from 10 to 4.

Fishermen now —! They had little and kept no hours. He would have liked to be a fisherman. He had watched them, once, on a holiday, from the ferry steps, taking the boats out, hoisting sail, and tacking, sometimes from one side of the harbour to the other, an hour, two hours – getting in. And out at sea, too, out at Sea!

Or a farm hand –. He would have liked to follow the plough. There was something about a furrow, the smell of the earth, the give of it under your feet, the brownness, the evenness, the everlastingness of it, up and down – which got hold of you like the sea; the smell and feel of the water, the blueness, the distance, the everlastingness of that. And then the horses, – the team of the plough. He could have lived with horses all his life. Sometimes he thought he would have liked to be an animal. Take cats for instance, – lying about, blinking and dozing; they had a secret worth knowing if it was only how to get all the heat and stillness and happiness out of the Sun.

Those men and animals he fancied had it, – the thing he hadn't got at, which was somehow in the sunshine and the night: in lights too, lamps along the winter streets, and shadows cutting across the parapets of the bridges.

Music would bring it; the band in the Green Park on Sunday evenings; and words from anywhere, in the pages of a newspaper – words like Victory and the Shepherd's Star and the South of France. There was another too which music brought in which for him loveliness had once been painted and blotted out, a woman's name. Everything about her had been dreamlike and a fragrance: and at first it was as pure loveliness he saw her, not a thing to touch, simply to wonder at; but later he would lie awake not sure if he could stand it if he didn't touch it; wishing that she would come to him through the night, and show him how to touch it; it was too bewildering alone.

One day he tried to say this to her, and it was difficult: she was arranging flowers. Suddenly he looked up and found she wasn't listening, and he had never wanted to speak to anyone about anything again.

And he had married Amy.

After that, as time went on, he came to have only one desire, – to be alone: but with Amy you could never be alone, even when she wasn't there: he hoped some day he should get used to her as he had got used to the scales and sovereigns at the Bank.

It was a month or so before his illness that it occurred to him he must have spent his life in sleep, because all at once, things were beginning to stand out for him in a new sort of daylight, so near that however far off they were he seemed almost able to touch them, and so clearly that he might have been looking at them through a pair of field-glasses.

And then one afternoon he discovered that there were only three things on this earth –: from the Bank steps, even from the house steps he found them in nearly everything except his street and over there, on the counter, in the notes and gold.

Everywhere else – and they were in remembered things, the bronze of the seaweed against the grey of the quay-wall; the sweep of a man's hand broadcasting along the furrow: the throb in the breasts of things that ought to be flying but could hardly hold their heads up in the boxes of the bird-shops.

A little while ago he had thought there were a hundred things but now he knew there were just these three which he was beginning to get hold of, and the place where they seemed to him most to be, all together, was in the fields. In the grass, the greenness, the wave of it in the wind, and the life in every blade.

And then he was struck down.

For weeks these women had rustled about the room, pouring stuff down his throat and talking about him in whispers behind a screen; and an Angel of God could not have got them out; but what chiefly worried him was being there shut in.

He broke free, in a way, by thinking of walks in bygone holidays, – before his marriage – the roads and the footpaths; and one day he asked Amy for the stick which had gone with him on which he had notched things in memory of the places, but she didn't bring it up.

The next day he asked her Mother for it who said 'Oh, I think she has given it to Tom' (Tom was Amy's brother) and after that when the Nurse came in to tell him how nicely he was getting on he laughed and took no notice of any one of them again.

He simply turned round and lay still and got over a stile into the fields and went on and on.

Sometimes it was Spring there and twilight was over them; he liked that best; but this morning it was the August sunshine and they were August fields.

Fields – fields, quite endless, mile after mile of gold, they were the real gold – the wheat stirring gently, with just above it the green, the line of the hedge and higher up, over it all the blue.

They were there, all three, the only things: the gold, the stir and the folded ear; they were in the wheat and his hand was passing over it and it was passing something into his hand.

All that there was or ever would be – he wanted to have it, to keep it: he was afraid of losing it; that was terror. It made him start up, it made him cry out almost as if he had seen them doing it – he didn't want them to cut down the wheat.

*Other Poems*

## In the Fields

Lord, when I look at lovely things which pass,
   Under old trees the shadows of young leaves
Dancing to please the wind along the grass,
   Or the gold stillness of the August sun on the August sheaves,
Can I believe there is a heavenlier world than this?
   And if there is
Will the strange heart of any everlasting thing
   Bring me these dreams that take my breath away?
They come at evening with the home-flying rooks and the scent of
                                                                                hay,
   Over the fields. They come in Spring.


## From a Window

   Up here, with June, the sycamore throws
   Across the window a whispering screen;
I shall miss the sycamore more, I suppose,
Than anything else on this earth that is out in green.
   But I mean to go through the door without fear,
   Not caring much what happens here
             When I'm away: –
How green the screen is across the panes
   Or who goes laughing along the lanes
   With my old lover all the summer day.

## Rooms

I remember rooms that have had their part
In the steady slowing down of the heart;
The room in Paris, the room at Geneva,
The little damp room with the seaweed smell
And that ceaseless maddening sound of the tide –
    Rooms where for good or for ill, things died:
But there is the room where we two lie dead
Though every morning we seem to wake, and might just as well seem
                                                        to sleep again
    As we shall some day in the other dustier quieter bed
    Out there – in the sun – in the rain.


## Monsieur Qui Passe
Quai Voltaire

A purple blot against the dead white door
In my friend's rooms bathed in their vile pink light,
I had not noticed her before
She snatched my eyes and threw them back to me:
She did not speak till we came out into the night,
Paused at this bench beside the kiosk on the quay.

God knows precisely what she said –
I left to her the twisted skein,
Though here and there I caught a thread, –
Something, at first, about 'the lamps along the Seine,
And Paris with that witching card of Spring
Kept up her sleeve, – why you could see

The trick done on these freezing winter nights!
While half the kisses of the Quay –
Youth, hope, – the whole enchanted string
Of dreams hung on the Seine's long line of lights.'

Then, suddenly she stripped, the very skin
Came off her soul, – a mere girl clings
Longer to some last rag, however thin,
When she has shown you – well – all sorts of things.
'If it were daylight – Oh! one keeps one's head –
But fourteen years! – No one has ever guessed –
The whole thing starts when one gets to bed –
Death? – If the dead would tell us they had rest –!
But your eyes held it as I stood there by the door –
One speaks to Christ – one tries to catch his garment's hem –
One hardly says as much to Him – no more:
It was not you, it was your eyes – I spoke to them.'

She stopped like a shot bird that flutters still,
And drops and tries to run again and swerves; –
The tale should end in some walled house upon a hill,
My eyes at least won't play such havoc there, –
Or hers –. But she had hair! blood dipped in gold;
And there she left me throwing back the first odd stare.
Some sort of beauty once, but turning yellow, getting old.
Pouah! These women and their nerves!
God! but the night *is* cold!

### Do Dreams Lie Deeper?

His dust looks up to the changing sky
        Through daisies' eyes;
    And when a swallow flies
        Only so high

73

He hears her going by
As daisies do. He does not die
In this brown earth where he was glad enough to lie.
But looking up from that other bed,
'There is something more my own,' he said,
'Than hands or feet or this restless head
That must be buried when I am dead.
The Trumpet may wake every other sleeper.
Do dreams lie deeper –?
And what sunrise
When these are shut shall open their little eyes?
They are my children, they have very lovely faces –
And how does one bury the breathless dreams?
They are not of the earth and not of the sea,
They have no friends here but the flakes of the falling snow;
You and I will go down two paces –
Where do they go?'


## Domus Caedet Arborem

Ever since the great planes were murdered at the end of the gardens
The city, to me, at night has the look of a Spirit brooding crime;
As if the dark houses watching the trees from dark windows
Were simply biding their time.


## Fin de Fête

Sweetheart, for such a day
One mustn't grudge the score;
Here, then, it's all to pay,
It's Good-night at the door.


74

Good-night and good dreams to you, –
    Do you remember the picture-book thieves
Who left two children sleeping in a wood the long night through,
    And how the birds came down and covered them with leaves?

So you and I should have slept, – But now,
    Oh, what a lonely head!
With just the shadow of a waving bough
    In the moonlight over your bed.

## Again

One day, not here, you will find a hand
Stretched out to you as you walk down some heavenly street,
You will see a stranger scarred from head to feet
But when he speaks to you you will not understand
Nor yet who wounded him nor why his wounds are sweet.
    And saying nothing, letting go his hand,
    You will leave him in the heavenly street –
              So we shall meet!

## Epitaph

    He loved gay things
    Yet with the brave
He laughed when he was covered with grey wings,
– Asking the darkest angel for bright things
    And the angel gave –
So with a smile he overstepped the grave.

## Friend, Wherefore –?

I will not count the years – there are days too –
    And to-night again I have said
'What if you should be lying dead?'
Well, if it were so, I could only lay my head
    Quietly on the pillow of my bed
  Thinking of Him on whom poor sufferers cried
  Suffering Himself so much before He died:
  And then of Judas walking three years by His side –
  How Judas kissed Him – how He was crucified.
        Always when I see you
          I see those two;
        Oh! God it is true
We do not, all of us, know what we do;
        But Judas knew.


## I so liked Spring

I so liked Spring last year
  Because you were here; –
    The thrushes too –
Because it was these you so liked to hear –
    I so liked you –

  This year's a different thing, –
    I'll not think of you –
But I'll like Spring because it is simply Spring
    As the thrushes do.

## Here Lies a Prisoner

Leave him: he's quiet enough: and what matter
Out of his body or in, you can scatter
The frozen breath of his silenced soul, of his outraged soul to the
winds that rave:
Quieter now than he used to be, but listening still to the magpie
chatter
Over his grave.


## May, 1915

Let us remember Spring will come again
To the scorched, blackened woods, where all the wounded trees
Wait, with their old wise patience for the heavenly rain,
Sure of the sky: sure of the sea to send its healing breeze,
Sure of the sun. And even as to these
Surely the Spring, when God shall please
Will come again like a divine surprise
To those who sit to-day with their great Dead, hands in their hands,
eyes in their eyes,
At one with Love, at one with Grief: blind to the scattered things and
changing skies.


## June, 1915

Who thinks of June's first rose to-day?
Only some child, perhaps, with shining eyes and rough bright
hair will reach it down
In a green sunny lane, to us almost as far away
As are the fearless stars from these veiled lamps of town.

77

What's little June to a great broken world with eyes gone dim
From too much looking on the face of grief, the face of dread?
      Or what's the broken world to June and him
Of the small eager hand, the shining eyes, the rough bright
                        head?


## Ne Me Tangito

'This man . . . would have known who and what
manner of woman this is: for she is a sinner.' –
                           S. Luke *vii. 39*


      Odd, *You* should fear the touch,
The first that I was ever ready to let go,
    I, that have not cared much
For any toy I could not break and throw
To the four winds when I had done with it, you need not fear the
                        touch,
Blindest of all the things that I have cared for very much
In the whole gay, unbearable, amazing show.

True – for a moment –: no, dull heart, you were too small,
Thinking to hide the ugly doubt behind that hurried puzzled little
                        smile:
Only the shade, was it, you saw? but still the shade of something vile:
              Oddest of all!
So I will tell you this. Last night, in sleep,
Walking through April fields I heard the far-off bleat of sheep;
And from the trees about the farm, not very high,
A flight of pigeons fluttered up into an early evening mackerel sky.
        Someone stood by and it was you:
        About us both a great wind blew.

78

My breast was bared
But sheltered by my hair
I found you, suddenly, lying there.
Tugging with tiny fingers at my heart, no more afraid:
The weakest thing, the most divine
That ever yet was mine,
Something that I had strangely made,
So then it seemed –
The child for which I had not looked or ever cared,
Of whom, before, I had never dreamed.


## Old Shepherd's Prayer

Up to the bed by the window, where I be lyin',
Comes bells and bleat of the flock wi' they two children's clack.
Over, from under the eaves there's the starlings flyin',
And down in yard, fit to burst his chain, yapping out at Sue I do hear
young Mac.


Turning around like a falled-over sack
I can see team ploughin' in Whithy-bush field and meal carts startin'
up road to Church-Town;
Saturday arternoon the men goin' back
And the women from market, trapin' home over the down.


Heavenly Master, I wud like to wake to they same green places
Where I be know'd for breakin' dogs and follerin' sheep.
And if I may not walk in th' old ways and look on th' old faces
I wud sooner sleep.

## *My Heart is Lame*

My heart is lame with running after yours so fast
        Such a long way,
Shall we walk slowly home, looking at all the things we passed
        Perhaps to-day?

Home down the quiet evening roads under the quiet skies,
        Not saying much,
You for a moment giving me your eyes
        When you could bear my touch.

But not to-morrow. This has taken all my breath;
        Then, though you look the same,
There may be something lovelier in Love's face in death
As your heart sees it, running back the way we came;
        *My* heart is lame.

## *On Youth Struck Down*
(From an unfinished elegy)

Oh! Death what have you to say?
'Like a bride – like a bride-groom they ride away:
You shall go back to make up the fire,
To learn patience – to learn grief,
To learn sleep when the light has quite gone out of your earthly
                              skies,
But they have the light in their eyes
        To the end of their day.'

## *The Trees are Down*

– and he cried with a loud voice:
Hurt not the earth, neither the sea, nor the trees –
(Revelation)

They are cutting down the great plane-trees at the end of the
gardens.
For days there has been the grate of the saw, the swish of the
branches as they fall,
The crash of trunks, the rustle of trodden leaves,
With the 'Whoops' and the 'Whoas,' the loud common talk, the loud
common laughs of the men, above it all.

I remember one evening of a long past Spring
Turning in at a gate, getting out of a cart, and finding a large dead rat
in the mud of the drive.
I remember thinking: alive or dead, a rat was a god-forsaken thing,
But at least, in May, that even a rat should be alive.

The week's work here is as good as done. There is just one bough
On the roped bole, in the fine grey rain,
Green and high
And lonely against the sky.
(Down now! –)
And but for that,
If an old dead rat
Did once, for a moment, unmake the Spring, I might never have
thought of him again.

It is not for a moment the Spring is unmade to-day;
These were great trees, it was in them from root to stem:
When the men with the 'Whoops' and the 'Whoas' have carted the
whole of the whispering loveliness away
Half the Spring, for me, will have gone with them.

It is going now, and my heart has been struck with the hearts of the
                planes;
Half my life it has beat with these, in the sun, in the rains,
     In the March wind, the May breeze,
In the great gales that came over to them across the roofs from the
                great seas.
     There was only a quiet rain when they were dying;
     They must have heard the sparrows flying,
And the small creeping creatures in the earth where they were lying –
     But I, all day, I heard an angel crying:
       'Hurt not the trees.'


## Smile, Death

Smile, Death, see I smile as I come to you
Straight from the road and the moor that I leave behind,
Nothing on earth to me was like this wind-blown space,
Nothing was like the road, but at the end there was a vision or a face
       And the eyes were not always kind.

   Smile, Death, as you fasten the blades to my feet for me,
On, on let us skate past the sleeping willows dusted with snow;
Fast, fast down the frozen stream, with the moor and the road and
              the vision behind,
  (Show me your face, why the eyes are kind!)
And we will not speak of life or believe in it or remember it as we go.

## The Rambling Sailor

In the old back streets o' Pimlico
On the docks at Monte Video
At the Ring o' Bells on Plymouth Hoe
He'm arter me now wheerever I go.
An' dirty nights when the wind do blow
I can hear him sing-songin' up from sea –:
Oh! no man nor woman's bin friend to me
An' to-day I'm feared wheer to-morrow I'll be,
Sin' the night the moon lay whist and white
On the road goin' down to the Lizard Light
When I heard him hummin' behind me.

'Oh! look, boy, look in your sweetheart's eyes
    So deep as sea an' so blue as skies;
An' 'tis better to kiss than to chide her,
If they tell 'ee no tales, they'll tell 'ee no lies
        Of the little brown mouse
        That creeps into the house
To lie sleepin' so quiet beside her.

'Oh! hold 'ee long, but hold 'ee light
Your true man's hand when you find him,
He'll help 'ee home on a darksome night
        Wi' a somethin' bright
        That he'm holdin' tight
In the hand that he keep behind him.

'Oh! sit 'ee down to your whack o' pies
So hot's the stew and the brew likewise
But whiles you'm scrapin' the plates and dishes,
A'gapin' down in the shiversome sea
For the delicate mossels inside o' we
Theer's a passel o' hungry fishes.'

At the *Halte des Marins* at *Saint Nazaire*
I cussed him, sittin' astride his chair;
An' Christmas Eve on the Mary Clare
I pitched him a'down the hatch-way stair.
But 'Shoutin' and cloutin's nothin' to me,
Nor the hop nor the skip nor the jump,' says he,
'For I be walkin' on every quay –'

*'So look, boy, look in the dear maid's eyes*
*And take the true man's hand*
*And eat your fill o' your whack o' pies*
*Till you'm starin' up wheer the sea-crow flies*
*Wi' your head lyin' soft in the sand.'*


## The Call

From our low seat beside the fire
    Where we have dozed and dreamed and watched the glow
  Or raked the ashes, stopping so
We scarcely saw the sun or rain
  Above, or looked much higher
Than this same quiet red or burned-out fire.
      To-night we heard a call,
    A rattle on the window-pane,
    A voice on the sharp air,
And felt a breath stirring our hair,
  A flame within us: Something swift and tall
Swept in and out and that was all.
Was it a bright or a dark angel? Who can know?
  It left no mark upon the snow,
    But suddenly it snapped the chain
    Unbarred, flung wide the door
    Which will not shut again;
And so we cannot sit here any more.

We must arise and go:
The world is cold without
And dark and hedged about
With mystery and enmity and doubt,
But we must go
Though yet we do not know
Who called, or what marks we shall leave upon the snow.


## *Absence*

Sometimes I know the way
You walk, up over the bay;
It is a wind from that far sea
That blows the fragrance of your hair to me.

Or in this garden when the breeze
Touches my trees
To stir their dreaming shadows on the grass
I see you pass.

In sheltered beds, the heart of every rose
Serenely sleeps to-night. As shut as those
Your guarded heart; as safe as they from the beat, beat
Of hooves that tread dropped roses in the street.

Turn never again
On these eyes blind with a wild rain
Your eyes; they were stars to me. –
There are things stars may not see.

But call, call, and though Christ stands
Still with scarred hands
Over my mouth, I must answer. So,
I will come – He shall let me go!

## *To a Child in Death*

You would have scoffed if we had told you yesterday
   Love made us feel, or so it was with me, like some great bird
      Trying to hold and shelter you in its strong wing; –
A gay little shadowy smile would have tossed us back such a solemn
                          word,
     And it was not for that you were listening
     When so quietly you slipped away
With half the music of the world unheard.
What shall we do with this strange summer, meant for you, –
     Dear, if we see the winter through
     What shall be done with spring?
This, this is the victory of the Grave; here is death's sting,
That it is not strong enough, our strongest wing.

But what of His who like a Father pitieth?
His Son was also, once, a little thing,
The wistfullest child that ever drew breath,
Chased by a sword from Bethlehem and in the busy house at
                          Nazareth
Playing with little rows of nails, watching the carpenter's hammer
                          swing,
Long years before His hands and feet were tied
And by a hammer and the three great nails He died,
      Of youth, of Spring,
Of sorrow, of loneliness, of victory the King,
        Under the shadow of that wing.

## Moorland Night

My face is against the grass – the moorland grass is wet –
My eyes are shut against the grass, against my lips there are the little
blades,
Over my head the curlews call,
And now there is the night wind in my hair;
My heart is against the grass and the sweet earth, – it has gone still, at
last;
It does not want to beat any more,
And why should it beat?
This is the end of the journey.
The Thing is found.

This is the end of all the roads –
Over the grass there is the night-dew
And the wind that drives up from the sea along the moorland road,
I hear a curlew start out from the heath
And fly off calling through the dusk,
The wild, long, rippling call –:
The Thing is found and I am quiet with the earth;
Perhaps the earth will hold it or the wind, or that bird's cry,
But it is not for long in any life I know. This cannot stay,
Not now, not yet, not in a dying world, with me, for very long;
I leave it here:
And one day the wet grass may give it back –
One day the quiet earth may give it back –
The calling birds may give it back as they go by –
To someone walking on the moor who starves for love and will not
know
Who gave it to all these to give away;
Or, if I come and ask for it again
Oh! then, to me.

## An Ending

You know that road beside the sea,
   Walled by the wavin' wheat,
Which winds down to the little town,
    Wind-blown and gray and up the crooked street?
       We'd used to meet
Just at the top, and when the grass was trodden down
       'Twas by our feet.
       We'd used to stand
And watch the clouds like a great fleet
   Sail over sea and over land,
      And the gulls dart
Above our heads: and by the gate
   At the road's end, when et was late
And all the ships was showing lights on quiet nights,
      We'd used to part.

So, Sir, you think I've missed my way,
   There's nothing but the Judgment Seat –
But ef I pray perhaps I may – what's that you say –
     A golden street?
   Give me the yellow wheat!
   Et edn't *there* we'm goin' to meet!
No, I'm not mazed, I make no doubt
   That ef we don't my soul goes out
'Most like a candle in the everlasting dark.
   And what's the odds? 'Twas just a spark
     Alight for her.
     I tell you, Sir,
That God He made et brave and plain,
   Sin' He knows better than yon Book
    What's in a look
You'd go to Hell to get again.

Another hour? An hour to wait –!
   I sim I'll meet her at the gate –
You know that road beside the sea –
   The crooked street – the wavin' wheat –?
(What's that? A lamp! Et made me start –)
   That's where our feet – we'd used to meet – on quiet nights –
My God! the ships es showing lights! –
        We'd used – to part.

# *Appendix*

Poems printed with the lines indented as in earlier versions

### *The Fête*

To-night again the moon's white mat
   Stretches across the dormitory floor
While outside, like an evil cat
   The *pion* prowls down the dark corridor,
Planning, I know, to pounce on me in spite
For getting leave to sleep in town last night.
But it was none of us who made that noise.
   Only the old brown owl that hoots and flies
Out of the ivy –; he will say it was us boys –
   *Seigneur mon Dieu!* the *sacré* soul of spies!
   He would like to catch each dream that lies
   Hidden behind our sleepy eyes;
Their dream? but mine –, it is the moon and the wood that sees;
All my long life how I shall hate the trees!

In the *Place d'Armes*, the dusty planes, all Summer through
Dozed with the market women in the sun and scarcely stirred
   To see the quiet things that crossed the square –
A tiny funeral, the flying shadow of a bird,
   The hump-backed barber, Célestin Lemaire,
   Old Madame Michel in her three-wheeled chair,
And filing past to vespers, two and two,
   The *demoiselles* of the *Pensionnat*
   Towed like a ship through the harbour bar
   Safe into port, where *le petit Jésus*

Perhaps makes nothing of the look they shot at you –:
   *Si, c'est défendu, mais que voulez-vous?*
It was the sun. The sunshine weaves
A pattern on dull stones: the sunshine leaves
   The portraiture of dreams upon the eyes
                 Before it dies.
              All Summer through
The dust hung white upon the drowsy planes
Till suddenly they woke with the Autumn rains.


      It is not only the little boys
        Who have hardly got away from toys,
   But I, who am seventeen next year
Some nights, in bed, have grown cold to hear
     That lonely passion of the rain
Which makes you think of being dead
And of somewhere living to lay your head
     As if you were a child again
Crying for one thing, known and near
Your empty heart to still the hunger and the fear
     That pelts and beats with it against the pane.


    But I remember smiling too
At all the sun's soft tricks and those Autumn dreads
   In Winter time when the grey light broke slowly through
The frosted window-lace to drag us shivering from our beds.
And when at dusk the singing wind swung down
Straight from the stars to the dark country roads beyond the
                           twinkling town,
Striking the leafless poplar boughs as he went by
   Like some poor stray dog by the wayside lying dead
   We left behind us the old world of dread
I and the wind as we strode whistling on under the Winter sky.

And then in Spring for three days came the Fair
   Just as the planes were starting into bud
Above the caravans: you saw the dancing bear
    Pass on his chain; and heard the jingle and the thud.
         Only four days ago
         They let you out of this dull show
To slither down the *montaine russe* and chaff the man *à la tête de*
                       *veau,* –
      Hit, slick, the bulls eye at the *tir,*
      Spin round and round till your head went queer
On the *porcs-roulants. Oh! là là! la Fête!*
*Va pour du vin! et le tête-à-tête*
With the girl who sugars the *gaufres! Pauvrette*
    How thin she was; but she smiled, you bet,
    As she took your tip – 'One does not forget
The good days, *Monsieur.*' Said with a grace
But *sacrebleu!* what a ghost of a face!
    And no fun too for the *demoiselles*
Of the *Pensionnat,* who were hurried past
    With their '*Oh, que c'est beau – Ah, qu'elle est belle!*'
A lap-dog's life from first to last!
The good nights are not made for sleep, nor the good days for
                       dreaming in,
And at the end in the big Circus tent we sat and shook and stewed
                       like sin!


    Some children there had got – but where?
Sent from the South, perhaps – a red bouquet
   Of roses sweetening the fetid air
With scent from gardens by some far away blue bay.
   They threw one at the dancing bear,
The white clown caught it. From St Rémy's tower
The deep, slow bell tolled out the hour;
   The black clown, with his dirty grin
   Lay, sprawling in the dust, as She rode in.

She stood on a white horse – and suddenly you saw the bend
   Of a far-off road at dawn, with Knights riding by –
A field of spears – and then the gallant day
Go out in storm, with ragged clouds low down, sullen and grey
   Against red heavens: wild and awful, such a sky
        As witnesses against you at the end
Of a great battle, bugles blowing, blood and dust –
The old *Morte d'Arthur*, fight you must –;
   It died in anger. But it was not death
   That had you by the throat stopping your breath,
She looked like Victory. She rode my way.

She laughed at the black clown and then she flew
       A bird above us on the wing
Of her white arms, and you saw through
   A rent in the old tent, a patch of sky
With one dim star. She flew, but not so high –
   And then – she did not fly –,
She stood in the bright moonlight at the door
Of a strange room –, she threw her slippers on the floor –
       Again, again,
   You heard the patter of the rain;
   The starving rain, it was this Thing,
Summer was this, the gold mist in your eyes –;
       Oh! God it dies.
       But after death?
  To-night the splendour and the sting
   Blows back and catches at your breath,
The smell of beasts, the smell of dust, the scent of all the roses in the
                world, the sea, the Spring –
The beat of drums, the pad of hoofs, music, the Dream, the Dream,
                the Enchanted Thing!

At first you scarcely saw her face,
You knew the maddening feet were there,
    What called was that half-hidden, white unrest
    To which now and then she pressed
    Her finger tips: but as she slackened pace
And turned and looked at you it grew quite bare:
There was not anything you did not dare: –
Like trumpeters the hours passed until the last day of the Fair.


In the *Place d'Armes* all afternoon
    The building birds had sung 'Soon, soon'
The shuttered streets slept sound that night,
               It was full moon:
The path into the wood was almost white,
The trees were very still and seemed to stare:
    Not far before your soul the Dream flits on,
    But when you touch it, it is gone
And quite alone your soul stands there.


Mother of Christ, no one has seen your eyes: how can men pray
               Even unto you?
    There were only wolves' eyes in the wood –
             My Mother is a woman too:
    Nothing is true that is not good
With that quick smile of hers, I have heard her say –:
I wish I had gone back home to-day,
I should have watched the light that so gently dies
From our high window, in the Paris skies,
    The long straight chain
    Of lamps hung out along the Seine:
I would have turned to her and let the rain
Beat on her breast as it does against the pane –:
    Nothing will be the same again –;
There is something strange in my little Mother's eyes.
There is something new in the old heavenly air of Spring –
The smell of beasts, the smell of dust –, *The Enchanted Thing!*

All my life long I shall see moonlight on the fern
And the black trunks of trees. Only the hair
   Of any woman can belong to God.
    The stalks are cruelly broken where we trod,
     There had been violets there.
     I shall not care
As I used to do when I see the bracken burn.


## Saturday Market

Bury your heart in some deep green hollow
    Or hide it up in a kind old tree
    Better still, give it the swallow
      When she goes over the sea.

In Saturday Market there's eggs a 'plenty
And dead-alive ducks with their legs tied down –
    Grey old gaffers and boys of twenty –
     Girls and the women of the town –
    Pitchers and sugar-sticks, ribbons and laces
    Posies and whips and dicky-birds' seed,
     Silver pieces and smiling faces,
In Saturday Market they've all they need.

What were you showing in Saturday Market
    That set it grinning from end to end
     Girls and gaffers and boys of twenty –?
    Cover it close with your shawl, my friend –
    Hasten you home with the laugh behind you,
       Over the down – out of sight,
    Fasten your door, though no one will find you,
     No one will look on a Market night.

See you, the shawl is wet, take out from under
The red, dead thing. In the white of the moon
On the flags does it stir again? Well, and no wonder –
    Best make an end of it, bury it soon.
    If there is blood on the hearth who'll know it?
        Or blood on the stairs,
    When a murder is over and done why show it?
    In Saturday Market nobody cares.


Then lie you straight on your bed for a short short weeping,
    And still for a long, long rest,
  There's never a one in the town so sure of sleeping
As you, in the house on the down, with a hole in your breast.


    Think no more of the swallow,
        Forget you, the sea,
    Never again remember the deep green hollow,
        Or the top of the kind old tree!


## Sea Love


Tide be runnin' the great world over:
    T'was only last June-month I mind that we
Was thinkin' the toss and the call in the breast of the lover
        So everlastin' as the sea.


    Heer's the same little fishes that sputter and swim;
Wi' the moon's old glim on the grey, wet sand;
    An' him no more to me nor me to him
    Than the wind goin' over my hand.

## May, 1915

Let us remember Spring will come again
To the scorched, blackened woods, where all the wounded trees
Wait, with their old wise patience for the heavenly rain,
Sure of the sky: sure of the sea to send its healing breeze,
Sure of the sun. And even as to these
Surely the Spring, when God shall please
Will come again like a divine surprise
To those who sit to-day with their great Dead, hands in their hands,
eyes in their eyes,
At one with Love, at one with Grief: blind to the scattered things and
changing skies.

# Abbreviations

The following abbreviations are used in the Notes and Textual Notes. Almost all quotations from Charlotte Mew's letters are made from the collection of them in Mary C. Davidow's unpublished Ph.D. thesis, checked against the originals where access to these was permitted.

Berg      The Berg Collection, the New York Public Library
BL4       British Library, Add. Mss. 57754
BL5       British Library, Add. Mss. 57755
Buffalo   Poetry/Rare Books Collection of the University Libraries of the State University of New York at Buffalo
CP        Charlotte Mew, *Collected Poems*, with a biographical memoir by Alida Monro, 1953
CPP       *Charlotte Mew: Collected Poems and Prose*, edited and with an Introduction by Val Warner, 1981
CPSP      *Charlotte Mew: Collected Poems and Selected Prose*, selected and edited by Val Warner, 1997
Davidow   Mary C. Davidow, 'Charlotte Mew: Biography and Criticism' (unpublished Brown University Ph.D. thesis), 1960
FB        Charlotte Mew, *The Farmer's Bride*, 1st edn, 1916, 2nd edn with eleven new poems, 1921
Fitzgerald Penelope Fitzgerald, *Charlotte Mew and her Friends*, 1984
Leighton  Angela Leighton, *Victorian Women Poets: Writing Against the Heart*, 1992
RS        Charlotte Mew, *The Rambling Sailor*, 1929
VW        Val Warner, 'New Light on Charlotte Mew,' *PN Review* 117, 1997, pp. 43–7

# *Notes*

## *Preface*

The 'case' for Mew is argued in the article of my own referred to under 'Criticism' in Further Reading.

Edith Sitwell's review was in the *Daily Herald* of 4 April 1921, and is quoted by Davidow on pp. 249–50 and 260. For the letter jointly signed by Hardy, Masefield and de la Mare, see Davidow, p. 345 and its note 91. May Sinclair's letter to Mew of 17 July 1913 is in the Berg Collection and on p. 301 of Davidow. Sinclair mentions Pound's sending three poems to *Poetry* (Chicago) in an undated letter, probably of around August 1913 (Davidow, p. 304). 'The Fête' was published in *The Egoist* in May 1914 and H.D.'s review of Mew's book in September 1916. The quoted words of Virginia Woolf's are in a letter of 9 November 1924 to Vita Sackville-West (*A Change of Perspective: The Letters of Virginia Woolf, Volume III, 1923–1928*, ed. Nigel Nicolson, London 1977, p. 140). The words can be read as referring to Hardy's opinion, not giving her own, but Woolf had also written admiringly of Mew's poetry in a letter of 25 January 1920 to R. C. Trevelyan (*The Question of Things Happening: The Letters of Virginia Woolf, Volume II, 1912–1922*, ed. Nigel Nicolson, London 1976, p. 419). Both letters are quoted by Warner (CPP p. xii). Sassoon's letter to Mew of 3 January 1924 is on p. 347 of Davidow. Mew replies on January 7 (Davidow p. 348), writing first of poems of Sassoon's own:

Pity and Beauty may be the divinest things but there is, too, something divine & wholesome & cleansing in righteous anger. You say Poets carry this present world on their shoulders. Well, if they do, it's load enough, & perhaps the only way of not letting it down is to hold it high. The other night I took up again *A Child's Garden of Verses* & came upon this:

> If I could find a higher tree,
> How much, much farther I could see.

But how long will it take the priests and politicians to get that into their heads? I suppose it's always more or less running in the poets' ears. You must please forgive this rigmarole – if you get to the end of it – & partly blame yourself for setting me on.

Sackville's review was printed in *The Bookman* of 21 December 1921. Henry Harland's letter to Mew of 3 January 1895 is on p. 279 of Davidow.

Marianne Moore's words can be found on p. 633 of *The Complete Prose of Marianne Moore*, ed. Patricia C. Willis (New York 1986).

For Warner's views about the dates at which Mew may have composed different parts of her writing, see CPSP, pp. xiv, xvi and xx.

## Table of Dates

The information here is drawn from Alida Monro's Memoir in CP, Warner's Introductions in CPP and CPSP, Davidow, Fitzgerald and VW. In CPSP and VW, Warner corrects one or two inaccuracies in the information in the other sources.

## Earlier Poems

It is not known at what dates Mew wrote many of her poems, so that there is something both arbitrary and provisional about the division of her poems in this edition: between, on the one hand, (1) 'earlier' poems, and, on the other hand, (2) poems in the first (1916) and second (1921) editions of *The Farmer's Bride*, (3) a short story included as a prose poem, and (4) other poems. This division should not be taken to mean that every poem in (2) and (4) is indubitably later than all of the poems in (1); and, certainly, poems in (4) are not indubitably later than poems in (2). Alida Monro, friend of Mew's and involved at the Poetry Bookshop in the publication of both the only volume of poems published in Mew's lifetime, *The Farmer's Bride*, and the posthumous volume, *The Rambling Sailor*, stated in 1953 that 'Few of the poems which were published posthumously in *The Rambling Sailor* (1929) were written after 1916 [the date of *The Farmer's Bride*]' (CP p. xx). At the end of *The Rambling Sailor* some 'Early Poems' were printed, but one of the poems in the main part of that book – 'Not for that City' – was written by 1902, and is therefore among this present book's Earlier Poems.

There would be arbitrariness in any division. But the division made here does respect the fact that some of the poems in *The Farmer's Bride* can be dated – none of them before 1912 – while many other poems can be given earlier dates. I hope readers may find it useful to have the division made, but they should bear in mind that Mew was probably already in her early thirties, or even older, when she wrote some of these 'earlier' poems (probably few, if any, of them are juvenilia), and that, where there is no external evidence of a poem's date, the division is based on judgement and not fact. (Clearly, too, where there is some evidence but it is indecisive, an element of judgement has entered.) The notes give what definite information there is about individual poems' dates of composition and first publication. Whenever the 'first publication' indicated is in book form, the words 'so far as is known' should be understood.

The following facts should probably be taken together with each other: as already stated, no poem in *The Farmer's Bride* is definitely earlier than 1912; letters of Mew's indicate that some of the poems in this volume can be dated between 1913 and 1915; Mew wrote, in a letter to Harold Monro of 14 December 1915, that the poems she wanted to include in it (those which in the event *were* included in it) 'hang together, for me, & mark a period' (Davidow p. 312, Buffalo ms.).

### 'There shall be no night there' In the Fields

First published in CPP. The quotation in the title is from Revelation 21:25.

### A Question

First published in CPP.

### Left Behind

First published in CPP. Warner suggests (VW p. 44) that John Donne's 'Batter my heart . . .', Holy Sonnet XIV, 'seems a likely influence', pointing out also that the first two words of his Holy Sonnet XV are the first two words of 'Left Behind'. There is evidence that Mew admired Donne's poetry: in a letter to Harold Monro of 3 January 1918 (Berg, not in Davidow), she copies out the first stanza of Donne's 'The Relique' and comments: 'if you don't know it, isn't it too lovely to miss?'

### A Farewell

First published in CPP. Compare Christina Rossetti's sonnet "Remember me when I am gone away'.

*Well, she too must have her day!*: Davidow (p. 367) compares Thomas Hardy's sonnet 'Her Reproach' (*Poems of the Past and the Present*, 1901), which ends: 'And over which the kindliest will but stay / A moment; musing, "He, too, had his day!"'

### V.R.I.

These two sonnets were first published, together, in *Temple Bar*, March 1901. *V.R.I.*: Victoria Regina Imperatrix, Victoria Queen and Empress.

### To a Little Child in Death

First published in *Temple Bar*, September 1901.

### At the Convent Gate

First published in *Temple Bar*, March 1902. Christina Rossetti had written 'The Convent Threshold', among other poems on the subject of the conflict between human and religious love. It is highly unlikely that Mew would not have known Rossetti's poems well, or that her reading of them would have had nothing to do with her writing a number of stories as well as poems both on this subject and on the subject of renunciation more generally. Leighton argues that in Mew's writing, prose as well as verse, there is 'an extraordinarily close re-writing of characteristic motifs' of Christina Rossetti (p. 280). For a case in which she sees a Mew poem as 'full of echoes' (p. 282) of a Rossetti poem, see the note below on '*Ne Me Tangito*'. Leighton points out (p. 271) that, as did Mew for most of her life, Rossetti lived in Bloomsbury, and was especially near the Mew family in her last years, before her death in 1894, after that family had made its move to Gordon Street in 1890. (This move had been dated 1888, but Warner points out in CPSP, p. ix, that the electoral roll shows this to be wrong.) Fitzgerald mentions (p. 37) that at one time Mew, with her mother and sister Anne, attended the same church as Rossetti.

### *Song* ('Oh! Sorrow, Sorrow, scarce I knew')

First published in *Temple Bar*, August 1902

### *Not for that City*

First published in *Temple Bar*, November 1902, though in RS not printed among 'Early Poems'. Fitzgerald (pp. 25–6) mentions that hanging in the Mews' homes was a picture by Mew's maternal grandfather, Henry Kendall, of a 'Shining City', started in connection with an architectural project of the family firm's but developed as a *dessin libre* and shown both at the Academy and (later) in the English section of the Paris Salon, 'where Baudelaire raved over it'. 'To the Mew children this was Jerusalem . . .' See also Mew's later poem, 'I Have Been Through the Gates'.

### *Afternoon Tea*

First published, among 'Early Poems', in RS.
*good five-o'clock people*: Compare Browning's 'Five o'clock Tea in a house we know' in his *Red Cotton Night-Cap Country*.

### *The Little Portress* (St Gilda de Rhuys)

First published in *Temple Bar*, July 1903. The poem could have been written any time after the holiday visit to the Breton convent that Mew made with some other women in 1901. She describes the visit in 'Notes in a Brittany Convent' (*Temple Bar*, October 1901), where she also writes at some length about the same 'little portress' (see CPP pp. 353–5). She ends the article with the paragraph: 'As one looks back there are so many scenes. Perhaps the most persistent is the picture of the little portress in her window, from which such very distant glimpses of the "world" and its "illusions" can come into view. She seems to borrow something from that stillness of the sunshine, in which, to memory, she always sits – a stillness which suspends the breath of question, like her spirit. "And the explanation of tranquillity is there!"' (CPP p. 355) The quotation of that final sentence is from the little portress's talk, in the conversation with her which Mew has described earlier.
**1st stanza**
*To waken . . . her face*: Compare the last lines of Tennyson's 'The Lady of Shalott':

> But Lancelot mused a little space;
> He said, 'She has a lovely face;
> God in his mercy lend her grace,
> > The Lady of Shalott.'

**2nd stanza**
*A thousand years of sun and shower*: Compare the first line of Wordsworth's untitled 'Lucy' poem: 'Three years she grew in sun and shower'.

**5th stanza**
*Soeur Marie de l'enfant Jésus*: Sister Mary of the infant Jesus.
*shadow-name*: Presumably the new name adopted by the portress on taking her vow.
*Beyond us to that golden bar*: Compare the opening of Dante Gabriel Rossetti's 'The Blessed Damozel':

> The blessed damozel leaned out
> From the golden bar of Heaven.

**6th stanza**
*Of prayer as exquisite as praise*: Compare (possibly) Wordsworth's 'The imperfect offices of prayer and praise', in Book 1 of *The Excursion* (line 216).


## Requiescat

First published in *The Nation*, 13 November 1909. If, as is possible, this was written only shortly before it was published, it is later than most of the other Earlier Poems. Compare Tennyson's poem with the same title, though it is only two quatrains long and more distinctly related than Mew's poem is to Wordsworth's 'Lucy' poems.
*Requiescat*: May he or she rest.


## Péri en Mer (Cameret)

First published in *The Englishwoman*, November 1913. Mew had briefly visited Camaret-sur-mer during a holiday in Brittany in 1909. Like *Requiescat*, but more certainly, this was written a number of years later than most of the other Earlier Poems. Both poems, together with the immediately following 'She was a Sinner', are poems it has been difficult to decide whether to place in this section or Other Poems.
*Péri en mer*: Lost at sea.
*where suddenly the light . . . Climbed home*: Compare (possibly) Wordsworth's

'when the light of sense / Goes out, but with a flash that has revealed / The invisible world . . .', in Book 6 of *The Prelude* (lines 600–602 in the 1850 version).
*Abri / De la Tempête*: Shelter from the storm.


### She was a Sinner

First published, among 'Early Poems', in RS. In the present edition the poem is placed last in Earlier Poems because it does not read as 'early' as most of the other ones. As elsewhere, Mew is here combining different 'Magdalene' and 'sinful woman' stories from the Gospels. The most definite reference, in the poem's last eight lines, is to the story in John 20:11–17:

But Mary [Magdalene] stood without at the sepulchre weeping: and as she wept, she stooped down, and looked into the sepulchre, and seeth two angels in white, sitting, the one at the head, and the other at the feet, where the body of Jesus had lain. And they say unto her, Woman, why weepest thou? She saith unto them, Because they have taken away my Lord, and I know not where they have laid him. And when she had thus said, she turned herself back, and saw Jesus standing, and knew not that it was Jesus. Jesus saith unto her, Woman, why weepest thou? whom seekest thou? She, supposing him to be the gardener, saith unto him, Sir, if thou have borne him hence, tell me where thou hast laid him, and I will take him away. Jesus saith unto her, Mary. She turned herself, and saith unto him, Rabboni; which is to say, Master. Jesus saith unto her, Touch me not; for I am not yet ascended to my Father: but go to my brethren, and say unto them, I ascend unto my Father, and your Father; and to my God, and your God.

But see also the reference to Mary Magadalene as a person 'out of whom [Jesus] had cast seven devils' (Mark 16:9) and, especially, the story of the woman who came to Jesus in the house of the Pharisee Simon, Luke 7:36–50 (quoted below in the note on the tenth stanza of 'Madeleine in Church'). Of this story, the first part of the poem could be a free, allegorical retelling from the woman's point of view, with the addition of references to Jesus' crown of thorns and crucifixion. See also Mew's poem '*Ne Me Tangito*'.

## *The Farmer's Bride* (1916)

The dedication-page of *The Farmer's Bride* reads:

> To—
> He asked life of Thee and Thou gavest him
> a long life: even for ever and ever.

Warner (CP p. xiv) conjectures that this dedication is to Charlotte Mew's brother Henry, who died in 1901 after spending the last years of his life confined as insane. Fitzgerald (p. 227) thinks it possible that the dedication is to Lucy Harrison, the headmistress at the school Mew had attended, who died on 13 April 1915. Mew had been passionately devoted to her teacher. The quotation is an adaption of verse 4 of Psalm 21. The same verse had been adapted by the poet's great-grandfather for his wife's grave.

### *The Farmer's Bride*

First published in *The Nation*, 3 February 1912. In a letter of 1926, Charlotte Mew noted that 'it is written in the English West Country dialect' (Davidow p. 353). Warner writes that the aunt Fanny whom Charlotte Mew would have met on annual childhood holidays on the Isle of Wight came from Crewkerne in Somerset, where there are two hamlets with the name of Churchtown (VW pp. 45–6).

This is the poem Alida Klementaski, later married to Harold Monro of the Poetry Bookshop, was 'electrified' by and committed to memory when (in her teens) she read it in *The Nation* (CP p. vii). Her subsequent repeating of it to Harold Monro led to the book of 1916 that has it as the title-poem.

Davidow (pp. 198ff.) relates the bride of this poem to the Sue Bridehead of Hardy's *Jude the Obscure* (1895). Readers of the novel will remember that for long periods this slim, dark-eyed and dark-haired character has no sexual relations with either her husband, Phillotson, or the lover, Jude Fawley, she leaves him for. She is described as shrinking from her husband's caresses, and in one episode, when he has agreed to sleep separately but one night forgets and enters her bedroom, she jumps out of the window. Earlier, she has fled the marital bedroom, then been found by Phillotson in a closet under the stairs: 'She looked so pitiful and pleading in her white night-gown against the shadowy lumber-hole that he was quite worried. She continued to beseech him not to disturb her' (Penguin Classics, 1998, p. 221). Later in the novel, she is living with Jude but sleeping separately, 'with only a landing between them' (p. 261), and later still Jude tells her that she is 'a sort of fay, or sprite – not a woman!' (p. 353). Another detail that may have lodged in Mew's mind is Phillotson's reference, when discussing with a friend Sue's request to be allowed to leave him for Jude, to the belief of most men that in such a case a wife should be put 'under lock and key' (p. 230). Mew's character is at the same time very different from Sue Bridehead. Among other things, the latter is highly articulate and has no special relations with animals. (The text of the Penguin Classics edition is based on that of the first publication of the novel in book form in 1895. Hardy later made some revisions, but all of the words quoted here are in all of the editions.)

In a letter of 10 July 1918 to Sydney Cockerell, Mew wrote:

I could only change my farmer by making him someone else – as, so far as I had the use of words, they did express my idea of a rough countryman seeing and saying things differently from the more sophisticated townsman – at once more clearly & more confusedly. I am afraid, too, that the point you touch on is more than merely technical – as it seems to me that in the 'cri de coeur' (I use your phrase) one either has or has not the person, & if the author is not right here he is wrong past mending – judged by Flaubert's implacable – 'Le mot ne manque jamais quand on possède l'idée' [The word never fails when one possesses the idea].

But as well as for your interesting criticism I have to thank you for turning my thoughts towards the test literature, of this 'cri de coeur'. In Marguerite Gautier's '*Je veux vivre*' [in the younger Dumas' *Dame aux camélias*] and Sarah Gamp's '*Drink fair, Betsy, wotever you do!*' [in Dickens' *Martin Chuzzlewit*] one has not only the cry but the gesture and the accent –. And so one goes on – calling up the witnesses to the 'real thing' & finds oneself in delightful company. (Davidow, p. 323, Berg ms.)

**1st stanza**
*fay*: Fairy.
**2nd stanza**
*Before our lanterns. To Church-Town*: In the dialect, 'To' can have the sense of 'At'.
**4th stanza**
*leveret*: Young hare.


## Fame

Written before 24 July 1913 when Mew in a letter to Edith Hill wrote: 'I am glad you like "Fame", which I personally prefer to anything I have done, though I don't know why' (Davidow p. 302, Buffalo ms.). First published in *The New Weekly*, 30 May 1914.

### The Narrow Door

First published in FB (1916).
**3rd stanza**
*Tiens! que veux-tu acheter?*: Well, well! what do you want to buy?
*Mais, pour quat'sous, des oignons*: I guess, for tuppence, I'll just take some onions.

### The Fête

Written 1913, first published in *The Egoist*, 1 May 1914. In a letter from Dieppe of 8 April 1914 to Ethel Oliver, Mew wrote:

the Square is a pure delight & when one hasn't too many holidays, it makes all the difference to be in the right place. And I should never have done the Fête verses if I hadn't been here last year. One realizes the place much more alone I think – it's all there is – & you don't feel it through another mind which mixes up things – I wonder if Art, as they say, is a rather inhuman thing –? anyhow, one can't choose the working of it – & here, I feel, even the sea for *seeing* things is a distraction, & if I do anything shall have to get away from it to some quiet place. (Davidow pp. 306–7, Buffalo ms.)

In the letter to Edith Hill of 24 July 1913 in which Mew writes about 'Fame', 'The Quiet House', 'Ken' and 'In Nunhead Cemetery', she goes on to write: 'The things now in my head are rather unmanageable, & possibly too big to pull off – as in this form I am really only a beginner' (Davidow p. 302, Buffalo ms.). The reference may well have been to 'The Fête', and also – possibly – to her first ideas for the poem that became 'Madeleine in Church'.
*Fête*: Fair.
**1st stanza**
*pion*: Auxiliary teacher.
*Seigneur Mon Dieu!*: Lord My God!
*sacré*: Blasted.
**2nd stanza**
*Place d'Armes*: Parade-Ground Square.
*demoiselles*: Young ladies.
*Pensionnat*: Private boarding-school, or hostel attached to a girls' *lycée*.
*le petit Jésus*: The infant Jesus.
*Si, c'est défendu, mais que voulez-vous?*: Yes, it's forbidden, but what do you expect?
**5th stanza**
*montaine russe*: Switchback.
*tête de veau*: Calf's head.

*tir*: Shooting-gallery.

*porcs-roulants*: Roundabout.

*Va pour du vin! et le tête-à-tête*: Go for some wine! and a tête-à-tête.

*gaufres*: Waffles.

*Pauvrette*: Poor little thing.

*sacrebleu!*: 'Strewth!

*Oh, que c'est beau – Ah, qu'elle est belle!*: Oh, isn't this beautiful! Ah, isn't she beautiful!

*The good nights are not made for sleep*: Compare Milton's *Comus* (lines 122–3):

> What hath night to do with sleep?
> Night hath better sweets to prove . . .

### 7th stanza

*Morte d'Arthur*: This is the title by which Sir Thomas Malory's collection of Arthurian stories is commonly known, and also the title of a poem by Tennyson.


## Beside the Bed

Written before 29 July 1913. First published in FB (1916).


## In Nunhead Cemetery

Written before 24 July 1913. First published in FB (1916). This cemetery is in south London and is where Mew's brother Henry was buried. In the letter to Edith Hill of 24 July 1913, Mew wrote of the last stanza of this poem: 'the last verse which you find superfluous is to me the most inevitable (– & was written first –) being a lapse from the sanity & self-control of what precedes it – The mind – & senses can stand no more – & that is to express their failure and exhaustion' (Davidow p. 302, Buffalo ms.).

### 5th stanza

*the Strand*: The well-known street in central London, starting from Trafalgar Square.

### 6th stanza

*Crystal Palace*: An outer suburb of south London.

### 8th stanza

*the lions in Trafalgar Square*: Sculpted lions at the foot of Nelson's Column.

### 12th stanza

*Though I am damned . . . where the starlings fly*: It seems likely that in some part of her mind Mew was remembering Dante's account, in Canto 5 of his

*Inferno*, of the damned lovers (or *peccator carnali*, 'carnal sinners' in Cary's translation). When these are first introduced, their being blown through the air by the tormenting wind is compared to how *gli stornei ne portan l'ali / nel freddo tempo* ('when winter reigns, / The starlings on their wings are borne abroad', Cary).

**14th stanza**
*I am scared, I am staying with you to-night*: Was this line anywhere in T. S. Eliot's mind when in *The Waste Land* (1922) he wrote, '"My nerves are bad to-night. Yes, bad. Stay with me . . ."'? Each of the two poets' lines makes both a sudden change into the present tense and a break in the rhythm. See also the note below on 'The Quiet House'.


### The Pedlar

First published in *The Englishwoman*, February 1914.


### Pécheresse

Written before 29 July 1913; first published in *The New Weekly*, 25 July 1914.
*Pécheresse*: Sinful woman.
**3rd and last stanzas**
*ma Doué*: In French *doué* means 'gifted'. Is the reference to her sailor-lover: 'my gifted guy'? Mew's French looks incorrect in having the feminine *ma* with the masculine *doué*.
**5th stanza**
*unshrived*: One who has not confessed, paid penance and received absolution.
**6th stanza**
With the last two lines compare (possibly) lines 267–70 of Alexander Pope's 'Eloisa to Abelard':

> I waste the Matin lamp in sighs for thee,
> Thy image steals between my God and me,
> Thy voice I seem in ev'ry hymn to hear,
> With ev'ry bead I drop too soft a tear.

Pope goes on developing the idea for another six lines. Mew may well have known, too, these lines from the heroine's long speech at the end of Act 1, Scene 3, of Jean Racine's *Phèdre*:

En vain sur les autels ma main brûlait l'encens:

Quand ma bouche implorait le nom de la déesse,

J'adorais Hippolyte; et, le voyant sans cesse,

Même aux pieds des autels que je faisais fumer,

J'offrais tout à ce dieu que je n'osais nommer.

## The Changeling

First published in *The Englishwoman*, 17 February 1913. In spite of the great differences, there is surely some relation between this poem and Christina Rossetti's 'Goblin Market'.

**4th stanza**

*The shy green grasses making love*: Mew originally wrote 'lush' for 'shy'. Writing on 18 January 1916 to Harold Monro, she says she is making the change because of Monro's suggestion that 'lush' was 'unsatisfactory' (Davidow p. 314, Buffalo ms.).

**5th stanza**

*the wold*: A wold is an upland area of open country.

## Ken

Written before 24 July 1913 when Mew in her letter to Edith Hill wrote: 'I wanted in "Ken" to do what you say I have done, i.e., obscure the tragic side by a gentleness of treatment' (Davidow p. 302, Buffalo ms.). First published in FB (1916).

**5th stanza**

The rhyme here of 'sits' and 'wits' is in Tennyson's 'Song – The Owl': 'Alone and warming his five wits, / The white owl in the belfry sits.'

## A Quoi Bon Dire?

First published in FB (1916).

*A Quoi Bon Dire?*: What's the good of saying?

## The Quiet House

Written before 24 July 1913 when Mew in her letter to Edith Hill wrote: 'and curious enough "The Quiet House" which you say you see objectively is perhaps the most subjective, to me, of the lot' (Davidow p. 302, Buffalo ms.). First published in FB (1916). Is there a relation between the fourth stanza of this poem and the opening lines of *The Waste Land*? See the note above on the 14th stanza of 'In Nunhead Cemetery'.

### On the Asylum Road

First published in FB (1916).

### Jour des Morts (Cimetière Montparnasse)

First published in FB (1916).
*Jour des Morts*: All Souls' Day.
*Cimetière Montparnasse*: Cemetery in Montparnasse, Paris.
*fête*: Name-day or birthday.

### The Forest Road

Written before 8 April 1914 when Mew in her letter to Ethel Oliver wrote: 'Dr Scott says the "Forest Road" was so deeply realized that it made him feel the writer was mad! a professional point of view.' (Davidow p. 306, Buffalo ms.) First published in FB (1916). Warner writes: 'Almost certainly drawing on information from Mew's contemporaries, Davidow stated "The Forest Road" was about her sister Freda, ten years younger than her, in a mental hospital on the Isle of Wight . . . The speaker leaves a disturbed loved woman at the asylum – unmentioned – perhaps for the first time' (VW p. 46).

### Madeleine in Church

Written 1914–15, first published in FB (1916). There is an indication that Mew found this poem difficult to finish: in a letter to her of 6 January 1915, May Sinclair wrote:

Finish – finish yr. Courtisan. She's magnificent. The last verses are all there – coiled up in a lobe of yr. brain asleep v waiting to be waked – just like darling Tommy in his basket.

Presently you'll hear them stirring in their sleep v soon after, the poem will finish itself. (Davidow p. 310, Berg ms.)

It is questionable, incidentally, whether 'Courtisan' is a quite accurate description of the poem's Magdalene. The poem may have been among the 'things now in my head' that Mew, in her letter to Edith Hill of 24 July 1913, describes as 'rather unmanageable, and possibly too big to pull off' (Davidow p. 302, Buffalo ms.; already quoted in the note on 'The Fête').

**1st stanza**

*As the far lights of everlastingness*: Compare Henry Vaughan's lines in 'The Retreat':

> But felt through all this fleshly dress
> Bright shoots of everlastingness.

**2nd stanza**

*his shining wedding face*: Compare Shakespeare's 'the whining schoolboy, with his satchel / And shining morning face' (*As You Like It*, II.vii).

*rips*: Slang for worthless or 'fast' people.

**4th stanza**

*and then blow down . . . . the street*: Compare from Tennyson's *Maud* (Part II lines 246–8):

> And the hoofs of the horses beat, beat,
> The hoofs of the horses beat,
> Beat into my scalp and my brain . . .

*If one had learned the trick*: Compare the last lines of Browning's 'Two in the Campagna':

> Where is the thread now? Off again!
> The old trick! Only I discern
> Infinite passion, and the pain
> Of finite hearts that yearn.

**6th stanza**

*Et avec ça – mais on a vécu, tout se paie*: And for all that – but one has lived, everything has its price.

**8th stanza**

*like any flock of baa-ing sheep*: Compare from Augusta Webster's dramatic monologue of a prostitute, 'A Castaway' (in her 1870 collection, *Portraits*):

> Why, if the worthy men who think all's done
> If we'll but come where we can hear them preach,
> Could bring us all, or any half of us,
> Into their fold, teach all us wandering sheep,
> Or only half of us, to stand in rows
> And baa them hymns and moral songs, good lack,
> What would they do for us? what could they do?

> Just think! with were't but half of us on hand
> To find work for . . . or husbands. Would they try
> To ship us to the colonies for wives?

Leighton points out the echo (p. 285). An earlier passage of 'A Castaway' can be compared with the 5th and 6th stanzas of 'Madeleine in Church':

> Well lit, tract!
> At least you've made me a good leaping blaze.
> Up, up, how the flame shoots! and now 'tis dead.
> Oh proper finish, preaching to the last –
> No such bad omen either; sudden end,
> And no sad withering horrible old age.
> How one would clutch at youth to hold it tight!
> And then to know it gone, to see it gone,
> Be taught its absence by harsh careless looks,
> To live forgotten, solitary, old –
> The cruellest word that ever woman learns.

## 9th stanza

*A handful of forgotten dust*: Compare any of (i) 'what's become of man's great extent and proportion, when himself shrinks himself, and consumes himself to a handful of dust?' (John Donne in the fourth of his *Devotions*); (ii) 'And my heart is a handful of dust' (Tennyson's *Maud*, Part II, line 241 – see the note above on Mew's 4th stanza); and (iii) 'the deceitful feeling that lures us on to joys, to perils, to love, to vain effort – to death; the triumphant conviction of strength, the heat of life in the handful of dust, the glow in the heart that with every year grows dim, grows cold, grows small, and expires – and expires, too soon, too soon – before life itself' (Joseph Conrad, *Youth*, 1902). The earlier line in this same stanza of Mew's poem, 'Why, this is awful, this is fear!', suggests the possibility that, together with one or more of (i) to (iii), Mew's stanza was in T. S. Eliot's mind when in *The Waste Land* he wrote: 'I will show you fear in a handful of dust.' See the references to *The Waste Land* in the earlier notes on 'In Nunhead Cemetery' and 'The Quiet House'.

## 10th stanza

*Mary*: Mew has combined the references in Luke 8:2 to 'Mary called Magdalene, out of whom went seven devils' and in Mark 16:9 to 'Mary Magdalene, out of whom [Jesus] had cast seven devils' with the story in the immediately preceding chapter of Luke, 7:36–50 (the identification of the unnamed woman here with Mary Magdalene is also in a poem and a picture of Dante Gabriel Rossetti's: 'Mary Magdalene at the door of Simon the Pharisee'):

And one of the Pharisees desired him that he would eat with him. And he went into the Pharisee's house, and sat down to meat. And, behold, a woman in the city, which was a sinner, when she knew that Jesus sat at meat in the Pharisee's house, brought an alabaster box of ointment, and stood at his feet behind him weeping, and began to wash his feet with tears, and did wipe them with the hairs of her head, and kissed his feet, and anointed them with the ointment. Now when the Pharisee which had bidden him saw it, he spake within himself, saying, This man, if he were a prophet, would have known who and what manner of woman this is that toucheth him: for she is a sinner. And Jesus answering said unto him, Simon, I have somewhat to say to thee. And he saith, Master, say on. There was a certain creditor which had two debtors: the one owed five hundred pence, and the other fifty. And when they had nothing to pay, he frankly forgave them both. Tell me therefore, which of them will love him most? Simon answered and said, I suppose that he, to whom he forgave most. And he said unto him, Thou hast rightly judged. And he turned to the woman, and said unto Simon, Seest thou this woman? I entered into thine house, thou gavest me no water for my feet: but she hath washed my feet with tears, and wiped them with the hairs of her head. Thou gavest me no kiss: but this woman since the time I came in hath not ceased to kiss my feet. My head with oil thou didst not anoint: but this woman hath anointed my feet with ointment. Wherefore I say unto thee, Her sins, which are many, are forgiven; for she loved much: but to whom little is forgiven, the same loveth little. And he said unto her, Thy sins are forgiven. And they that sat at meat with him began to say within themselves, Who is this that forgiveth sins also? And he said to the woman, Thy faith hath saved thee; go in peace.

### Exspecto Resurrectionem

First published in FB (1916).
*Exspecto Resurrectionem*: I await, or look for, the Resurrection. The words are from the Nicene Creed in the Roman Missal's Order of High Mass. In a brief tavern scene in Thomas Hardy's *Jude the Obscure* (1895), Jude recites in Latin these and other words from that Creed (Penguin Classics, p. 122). See the note above on 'The Farmer's Bride'.

## Poems added in the second edition of *The Farmer's Bride* (1921)

### On the Road to the Sea

First published in *The Englishwoman*, June 1914. On 13 April 1919, Florence Hardy wrote to Mew that they, presumably including her husband, Thomas

Hardy, as well as some Cambridge friends, among them Lowes Dickinson and E. M. Forster, had been reading this poem 'with *great* appreciation' but having 'a never-ending controversy' between them as to whether the speaker in it is a man or a woman. All the men thought it was a woman, while she and another woman thought it was a man (Davidow p. 332, Berg ms.). Mew replied next day: '*The Road to the Sea* presents to me a middleaged man speaking – in thought – to a middleaged woman whom he has only met once or twice. – This last week there has been a suggestion of another edition of the *Farmer's Bride* & if the *Road to the Sea* went into it, perhaps it would make it clearer – (or darker) if this were put at the head of it: "La beauté des jeunes femmes est distribuée sur les diverses parties de leur corps \*\*\* mais cette beauté, quand elles vieillissent, se fixe toute sur leur visage."' (Davidow pp. 332–3, Berg ms. The beauty of young women is spread out on the various parts of their body . . . but this beauty, when they grow old, fixes itself all on their face.) I have not discovered the source of the quotation in French. Florence Hardy noticed that when the 1921 *Farmer's Bride* came out Mew had altered certain lines in this 'perhaps my favourite of all your poems,' and made the speaker's gender certain (Davidow p. 339, Berg ms.). In the text in *The Englishwoman*, the second line has 'others' instead of 'other women'. Further differences here, besides some differences in punctuation and line-indentation, are: in line 7 the 'my' of 'my gathering' is italicized; the last line of the second stanza has 'because you' instead of 'and you'; in the third stanza 'face', 'thought' and 'dream' all begin with capital letters, and it is 'how vile' instead of 'so vile'; in the fourth stanza, 'tell me' has a question-mark after it, and instead of 'how vain to ask', (but not in brackets) 'How hideous to ask!', and then the last line has 'were small' instead of 'are small'; in the seventh stanza there are no brackets around the last two lines.

### The Sunlit House

Written before 29 July 1913, first published in FB (1921).

### The Shade-Catchers

First published in FB (1921).

### Le Sacré-Coeur (Montmartre)

First published in FB (1921). The white, domed church of *Le Sacré-Coeur* (the Sacred Heart) is on a hill that overlooks the famous Montmartre nightlife district of Paris.

**1st stanza**
*Une jolie fille à vendre, très cher*: A pretty girl for sale, very dear.
**2nd stanza**
'*I thirst.*': From the account of the Crucifixion in John (19:28).
*cela peut se croire*: One can believe that.
*c'est la mer à boire*: It's like having the sea to drink.
*mais comme c'est vieux*: But how old it is.
*On ne peut pas toujours pleurer les morts*: One can't always be weeping over the dead.

### Song ('Love Love to-day, my dear')

First published in *The Athenaeum*, 24 October 1919. In a letter to Sydney Cockerell of 28 August 1919, Mew wrote that this poem was 'written for music, & not quite 20th century!' and 'perhaps I shall one day put an air to it' (Berg).
Compare the second half of the first stanza with John 3:8: 'The wind bloweth where it listeth, and thou hearest the sound thereof, but canst not tell whence it cometh, and whither it goeth: so is every one that is born of the Spirit.'

### Saturday Market

First published in FB (1921). When the second edition of *The Farmer's Bride* was published in the US, this poem became its title-poem.
**2nd stanza**
*gaffers*: Elderly countrymen.
*posies*: Bouquets or bunches of flowers.
**4th stanza**
*flags*: Flagstones.

### Arracombe Wood

First published in FB (1921).
*Arracombe Wood*: If, as is likely, this is a real and not a fictional wood, I have not been able to discover where it is.

*bird-witted*: The *OED* entry indicates that this phrase means something more specific than simply 'weak in the head'. It means a lack of the faculty of attention.

*there baint no mem'ry*: There isn't any memory.

*'Will be*: There will be.

*whizzle*: Whistle.


### Sea Love

First published in Number 1 of the Poetry Bookshop's *The Chapbook*, July 1919.

*glim*: Light.


### The Road to Kérity

First published in FB (1921). Kérity is a small fishing-port in Brittany.


### I Have Been Through the Gates

First published in Number 13 of *The Chapbook*, July 1920. See the earlier note on Mew's poem 'Not for that City'. The Christminster (or Oxford) that from a distance is a vision of spires and domes and lofty wisdom for the hero of Thomas Hardy's *Jude the Obscure* (1895) and then, after he goes there, a matter for deep personal disappointment and disillusion is, early in the novel, 'likened to the new Jerusalem' by Jude (Penguin Classics, p. 22). See references to Hardy's novel in the earlier notes on 'The Farmer's Bride' and '*Expecto Resurrectionem*'.

*they are empty; darkness is over them*: A typescript and corrected proof, both at Buffalo, show that Mew originally wrote 'and' before 'darkness'. Did that sound more in the style of the Authorized Version than she finally wanted?

*Over which Christ wept*: See Luke 19:41–4.


### The Cenotaph

First published in *The Westminster Gazette*, 7 September 1919.

*God is not mocked*: Galatians 6:7: 'Be not deceived; God is not mocked: for whatsoever a man soweth, that shall he also reap.'

## The Wheat

First published in *Time and Tide*, 20 February 1954. All the following notes except for the note on the third paragraph record alterations made by Mew on a typescript in BL4.

**2nd paragraph**

*which he hadn't got at and that other sense*: In the BL4 typescript 'with it,' follows 'and' and has a ms. line through it.

**3rd paragraph**

*handing out gold across the counter*: Clearly much of the money was in coin and not note form. Hence the later reference to 'the scales' on the counter.

**4th paragraph**

*They had little*: 'They had very little' in BL4, with a line through 'very'.

**5th paragraph**

*Take cats for instance*: 'Take cats and dogs for instance, –' in BL4, with a line through 'and dogs'.

*blinking and dozing*: 'blinking and dozing in the sunshine;' in BL4, with a line through 'in the sunshine'.

**7th paragraph**

*in the pages*: 'the pages' in BL4, with 'in' added in ms.

*Shepherd's Star*: A ms. substitution for 'Rambling Sailor' in BL4.

*for him loveliness had once been painted and blotted out*: In BL4 'all' comes between 'him' and 'loveliness', but with ms. brackets round the word, seeming to indicate that deletion was being considered by Mew; 'blotted out' is a ms. substitution for 'shut away'.

*Everything about her had been*: 'had been' is a ms. substitution for 'was'.

*and show him how to touch it*: After 'it' BL4 has 'or some other way to stand it', with a line through the words.

**8th paragraph**

*One day he tried to say this*: After 'say' BL4 has 'all', with a line through it.

*and he had never wanted*: BL4 has 'all his life' after 'and', with ms. brackets round the words; 'had' is a ms. addition.

**10th paragraph**

*used to her*: 'her' is a ms. substitution for 'it'.

**12th paragraph**

*nearly everything except his street*: In BL4 'except' is followed by 'in the pavement stones of his street', with a line through the words 'the pavement stones of' and a ms. bracket before them.

**13th paragraph**
*Everywhere else – and they were*: The last two words are ms. additions in BL4.
**14th paragraph**
*In the grass*: In BL4 a new paragraph starts here but a ms. line cancels that.
**17th paragraph**
*broke free*: 'broke' is a ms. substitution for BL4's 'got'.
*gone with him*: BL4 has a cancelled comma after these words.
**18th paragraph**
*for it*: A ms. addition in BL4.
*Amy's*: a ms. substitution for 'her'.
**21st paragraph**
*they were the real gold – the wheat*: A ms. addition in BL4, where this paragraph is followed by the short cancelled one: 'And again below, the gold (this was the real gold) the wheat'.
**23rd paragraph**
*that was terror*: BL4 originally read 'it was like a terror'. A ms. 'that' replaces 'it'; a ms. 'a sort of' replaces 'like a' and then has a line through it.


## Other Poems

### In the Fields

First published in *The Sphere*, March 1923.


### From a Window

First published in RS.
*How green the screen is*: In a Buffalo corrected typescript, 'is' is a ms. substitution for 'the sycamore throws'.


### Rooms

First published in RS.
*In the steady slowing down of the heart*: In a BL5 corrected typescript of this poem, 'slowing down' is a ms. substitution for 'wearing out'.
*the room where we two lie dead*: In BL5, 'two' is in parentheses. Warner (CPSP pp. xxii–xxiii) plausibly conjectures that Mew's typist was here following Mew's manuscript, where the parentheses would probably have indicated that she was considering deleting the word. Did the typist's 'error' lead Mew

to put a line through the whole typescript, as Warner further conjectures, or did she leave it uncorrected because she had still not decided about the possible deletion?

*dustier quieter*: A ms. substitution in BL5 for what appears to be 'narrower'.

### Monsieur Qui Passe (Quai Voltaire)

First published in RS. The Quai Voltaire is in Paris, running along the Left Bank of the Seine between the Pont du Carrousel and the Pont Royal.

*Monsieur Qui Passe*: A passing gentleman.

**3rd stanza**

*a mere girl clings*: In a BL5 typescript of this poem, 'girl' is a ms. substitution for the same word in French, *fille*.

*One speaks to Christ – one tries to catch his garment's hem*: The Gospel story of the sick woman coming behind Jesus, touching the hem of his garment and being healed, though not speaking to him until he asks who has touched him (Luke 8:43–8), seems to be combined here with 'Magdalene' stories in the Gospels. See the notes above on 'She was a Sinner' and the tenth stanza of 'Madeleine in Church'.

### Do Dreams Lie Deeper?

First published in RS.

### Domus Caedet Arborem

First published in RS.

*Domus Caedet Arborem*: The house kills the tree. (*Caedet* can also mean 'cuts down'.)

### Fin de Fête

First published in *The Sphere*, 17 February 1923.

*Fin de Fête*: End of the party, festivities or festival.

### Again

First published in RS. In a Buffalo corrected typescript, 'some' is a ms. substitution for 'the' (before 'heavenly street').

### Epitaph

First published in RS.

### Friend, Wherefore –?

First published in RS.
*We do not, all of us, know what we do*: Luke, 23:34: 'Then said Jesus, Father, forgive them; for they know not what they do.'

### I so liked Spring

First published in RS.

### Here Lies a Prisoner

First published in RS.
*The frozen breath*: In a Buffalo corrected typescript, 'breath' is a ms. substitution for (or correction of?) 'wealth'.

### May, 1915

Dated 23 May 1915, both in a Buffalo manuscript and in a BL5 typescript. First published in RS. In the manuscript the poem's title is 'Spring 1915' and there are two places in line 3 where the words are different: 'Wail' instead of 'Wait' and 'the old wise' instead of 'their old wise'. Mew could well have changed the poem's title after writing 'June, 1915'.

### June, 1915

First published in RS.

### Ne Me Tangito

First published in RS. The title seems to be the 'Touch me not' of John 20:17, said by the risen Christ to Mary Magdalene in the garden of the empty sepulchre. In the Vulgate, the Latin is *Noli me tangere*, and it is not known how Mew came to use her different Latin words. The poem's epigraph is (with words omitted) from a different Gospel story, Luke 7:36–50, quoted above in the note on the tenth stanza of 'Madeleine in Church'.

*Odd*, You *should fear the touch*: In the story in Luke 7, it is the Pharisee Simon who believes that Jesus ought to have feared the touch of the sinful woman washing his feet with her tears, drying them with her hair, and kissing and anointing them. In a story in Luke 8, of the sick woman behind Jesus touching the hem of his garment, Jesus says, 'Who touched me? . . . Somebody hath touched me: for I perceive that virtue is gone out of me.'

*the far-off bleat of sheep*: Compare Christina Rossetti's 'far-off piteous bleat of lambs and sheep' in her sonnet 'On the Wing'. Like Mew's, this poem describes a dream, and this dream includes a field, flying pigeons and a wind as well as the bleating lambs and sheep. Leighton argues (pp. 281–3) for a peculiarly close and interesting relation between the two poems.

### Old Shepherd's Prayer

First published in RS.
**1st stanza**
*clack*: Loud talking.
**2nd stanza**
*Whithy-bush*: Probably willow.
*meal*: The edible part of grain.
*Church-Town*: Compare the mention of this place in the second stanza of 'The Farmer's Bride'. There are two villages of this name in Somerset.
*trapin'*: Tramping, trudging.

### My Heart is Lame

First published in RS.

### On Youth Struck Down (From an unfinished elegy)

First published in RS.

### The Trees are Down

First published in Number 33 of *The Chapbook*, January 1923. Fitzgerald (p. 187) refers to speculators beginning to clear the south side of Euston Square Gardens in 1922, just at the top of Gordon Street where the Mews lived from 1890 to 1922. The poem's epigraph is from Revelation 7:2–3. Though the subject of the felling of loved trees is differently handled in each poem, compare William Cowper's 'The Poplar-Field', and also (possibly) Gerard Manley Hopkins' 'Binsey Poplars' (first published 1918).

**5th stanza**
*Half my life*: Thirty-two of the fifty-three years Mew had lived in 1922.

### Smile, Death

First published in RS. This poem and 'Moorland Night' are perhaps the poems of Mew's that show the clearest signs of her enthusiasm for Emily Brontë's poetry. She wrote an essay on it and submitted it to the publisher Elkin Matthews, with the idea that it could be 'an introduction to a separate re-publication of her poems' (Mew's words, Davidow p. 285). The idea was turned down but the essay was published in *Temple Bar*, August 1904, and also in CPP. In CPP, Warner also prints 'Elinor', a story of Mew's that had apparently never been printed before. She includes the story, too, in her CPSP and suggests there (p. xxi) that its main character is a 'fictionalised' Emily Brontë. A BL5 corrected typescript of this poem differs in a few words from the text published in the posthumous *The Rambling Sailor*, but this published version is what is printed here since it must very likely have been based on another (and later?) typescript, now unknown. The variations recorded below may have been Mew's earlier thoughts.

*see I smile*: 'I shall smile' BL5.

*that I leave behind*: 'I must leave behind', BL5.

*on earth to me*: 'on this great earth', BL5.

*this wind-blown space*: 'that wind-blown space', BL5.

*but at the end*: 'but at the end of it', BL5.

*the sleeping willows*: 'long low hedges', BL5. There is no punctuation at the end of this line in the typescript.

*with the moor and the road*: 'with the moon and the road', BL5.

Line 9 No brackets in BL5.

### The Rambling Sailor

First published in Number 25 of *The Chapbook*, February 1922. The stanzas in italics have always been printed thus (except in CPSP, where by mistake the last stanza is in Roman). The same speaker's words in the last three lines of the poem's penultimate stanza are presumably not in italics because spoken rather than sung.

**1st stanza**

*Pimlico*: The Thames-side inner London district, just west of Westminster.

*sing-songin'*: The *OED* gives as a meaning of this verb 'to force by means of singing', as well as to utter in a monotonous chant.

**4th stanza**

*whack*: Large quantity.

*mossels*: Morsels.

*passel*: Parcel in the dialect sense of a large number.

**5th stanza**

*Halte des Marins*: Sailors' rest.

*Saint Nazaire*: Large port on the Atlantic coast of France.


### The Call

First published, in a different version and under the title 'The Voice', in *The Englishwoman*, March 1912.

*Or raked the ashes, stopping so*: In 'The Voice', it is 'stooping', not 'stopping', and the lines immediately following are:

> We scarcely saw the sun and rain
>> Through the small curtained window-pane,
>>> Or looked much higher
> Than this same quiet red or burned out fire,
>> To-night we heard a call,
>> A voice on the air,

*It left no mark upon the snow*: 'The Voice' has 'made' instead of 'left'.

*But suddenly it snapped the chain*: 'The Voice' has 'But suddenly, in passing, snapped the chain,'.

*We must arise and go*: Compare the words of the parable's Prodigal Son, 'I will arise and go to my father' (Luke 15:18), and the first line of Yeats's 'The Lake Isle of Innisfree', 'I will arise and go now, and go to Innisfree . . .' (*The Rose*, 1893).


### Absence

First published in RS.

**3rd stanza**

*as safe as they . . . in the street*: Compare the lines in the fourth stanza of 'Madeleine in Church' and the quotation from Tennyson's *Maud* in the note on them.

### To a Child in Death

First published in *The Bookman*, April 1922.

### Moorland Night

First published in *The Nation and Athenaeum*, 24 January 1925.

### An Ending

First published in CPP. Davidow (p. 365n.) and Warner (CPSP p. xviii and VW p. 45) report that a manuscript of this poem in the possession of a family Mew had known from her schooldays was believed in that family to date from the early 1890s. That may be right, though the character and quality of the poem make it difficult to accept a date so early. No other poem in dialect can be definitely dated before 1912, and no other poem where the lengths of the lines are varied so much – or so sensitively, as in the lengthening of the fourth line here:

> Et edn't *there* we'm goin' to meet!
> No, I'm not mazed, I make no doubt
> That ef we don't my soul goes out
> 'Most like a candle in the everlasting dark.

The treatment of death has more in common with that in 'In the Fields' (first published in 1923) and 'Old Shepherd's Prayer' (first published in 1929), and in the story 'The Wheat' (which Warner thinks was 'probably' written about 1915, CPSP p. xvi, and I think could have been even later), than with the treatment of death in 'Not for that City' (first published in 1902). In the poem's second stanza the following of 'golden street' by 'yellow wheat' in the next line may suggest knowledge of the *Centuries of Meditation* by the seventeenth-century writer, Thomas Traherne. The third section of 'The Third Century' begins: 'The corn was orient and immortal wheat, which never should be reaped, nor was ever sown. I thought it had stood from everlasting to everlasting. The dust and stones of the street were as precious gold . . .' (This is quoted from the text as it was first put into print in 1908, modernized, by Bertram Dobell.) Perhaps the play on gold and wheat in Mew's story/prose-poem 'The Wheat' further strengthens the possibility that she had read the Traherne.

**2nd stanza**

*A golden street*: Compare 'the street of the city was pure gold' in Revelation 21:21. The golden street (or streets) is mentioned in two consecutive poems in Christina Rossetti's set of poems on 'The New Jerusalem and its citizens': the poems beginning 'The joy of Saints, like incense turned to fire' and 'What are these lovely ones, yea, what are these?'.

*mazed*: Mad.

*'Most*: Almost.

**3rd stanza**

*sim*: Seem.

# Textual Notes

The texts in the previous editions of Mew's poems, from *The Farmer's Bride* onwards, have been compared both with texts in original manuscripts and typescripts, where these exist and access to them was permitted, and with the texts of poems as first printed in papers and magazines. Easily the greatest number of the discrepancies are only in the punctuation and the line-indentations, not the words. There are also a few discrepancies in the use of capital letters at the beginnings of words. Since an editor's textual decisions between the different versions of some of these poems are difficult ones and cannot be completely satisfactory, as I explain briefly below, it is fortunate that, by and large, these decisions are of no great consequence. (Where manuscripts and typescripts show Mew herself changing any words, this is already recorded in the Notes above.)

My initial assumption was that, since the 1916 first edition and 1921 second edition of *The Farmer's Bride* were printed in Mew's lifetime, with Mew certainly correcting the proofs herself in 1916, there would be little case for restoring any older readings in the poems included in those two editions. But that assumption has not survived the closer attention to the punctuation and line-indentations that editing this book has involved me in. Alida Monro of the Poetry Bookshop wrote that, as Mew 'herself always declared to be the case', she 'hadn't the faintest idea how to punctuate', and 'gave the present writer *carte blanche* to correct the punctuation of her poems as she might think fit' (CP p. xvii). Mew's declaration and *carte blanche* may, however, have been due to her special diffidence, of which there are several stories: for example, her original reply to the suggestion of the Poetry Bookshop's publishing a book of her poems, that no one would want to read them (CP p. vii); or her saying, on first coming into that Bookshop and being asked whether she was Charlotte Mew, 'I am sorry to say I am' (CP p. viii). On the other hand, it must be admitted that letters of Mew's to Harold Monro do show that she could also express strong wishes about how the poems should be printed.

I believe the poetry gains, however slightly, from the lighter punctuation that sometimes, though not frequently, marks texts that preceded first publication in book form; and that it also gains from the evident fondness Mew had for punctuating with a dash, both instead of other punctuation and, especially, in combination with a full stop, a colon, a semi-colon, a question-mark, an exclamation-mark or a comma. The dash may precede or follow the other punctuation, but her special fondness is for having it precede. (When Nicholson Baker, towards the end of his essay on 'The History of Punctuation' (collected in *The Size of Thought*, New York 1996), writes of how the use of a dash after another piece of punctuation has more or less disappeared in the twentieth century, he states that the 'variant' on this of a dash preceding a comma is 'extremely rare' and makes no mention at all of a dash preceding any other punctuation.) Two small examples of the gain of restoring lighter punctuation can be found in 'The Cenotaph': the phrases 'the wild, sweet, blood of wonderful youth' and 'the small, sweet, twinkling country things' in the editions from FB (1921) onwards did not, when the poem was first printed in *The Westminster Gazette*, have any of their commas. To my ear and feeling, they are better without them. Mew's fondness for combining a dash with another piece of punctuation was shown when she corrected the proof of 'I Have Been Through the Gates' for *The Chapbook* (the corrected proof is in Buffalo) and deliberately changed to a dash followed by a semi-colon the comma which in the proof and in an original typescript (also at Buffalo) follows line 2's 'dreams'. An example of the subsequent 'correcting' of this kind of punctuation, and probably not by Mew herself, is that, while in a Buffalo typescript of 'Moorland Night' the 2nd stanza's line 6 ends, after 'rippling call', with a dash followed by a colon, this was first changed to a colon followed by a dash in *The Nation and the Athenaeum*, then to a simple full stop in the 1929 posthumous collection, *The Rambling Sailor*. With poems published in book form only after Mew's death, the argument is, of course, even stronger for restoring older readings.

I have no general explanation of the changes made to original line-indentations, but in at least one kind of example there may have been a slight loss here, too, from later editing. This is where an original manuscript or typescript places a suddenly much shorter line at the very centre of the page, to some expressive effect, as with the second line of 'The Changeling', but this is then, when the poem is printed, moved further towards the left-hand margin. Though this kind of example has tempted me to restore all the older line-indentations that we have in original manuscripts or typescripts, it remains unclear how these came to be changed, and since the three poems most affected were all in *The Farmer's Bride*, published in Mew's lifetime, it seems preferable to print only in an Appendix – for the interested reader – texts based in this respect on the Buffalo typescript of 'The Fête', on the corrected Buffalo manuscript of 'Sea Love' and on the Buffalo manuscript of 'Saturday Market'. Perhaps the most interesting inclusion in this Appendix is 'Saturday Market', which looks much less like a ballad on the pages of Mew's manuscript. Also in this Appendix is the text of a BL5 corrected typescript of 'May, 1915'. It is possible, of course, that, when the Poetry Bookshop published this poem in the posthumous *Rambling Sailor* volume, the line-indentations were changed so much because the publishers had another, now lost typescript.

The original editions, FB and RS, and also CP, were printed with each poem's first letter a large one, stretching down to the second line and clearly, in many cases, pushing over that second line further to the right, but making it difficult to determine the exact amount of indentation, if any, Mew intended for it. Warner has a number of changes of mind here between her two editions, CPP and CPSP.

I suspect that Mew's decisions about the indentations of lines were determined by the aesthetic consideration of the appearance of the lines on the page as well as by considerations of immediate expressiveness.

I should finally emphasize that little or nothing is known about the exact status of the manuscripts and typescripts I have consulted and often drawn on. Many may be presumed to be Mew's final texts, but that is no more than a presumption: they do not necessarily have a greater authority than even the Poetry Bookshop's RS, let alone FB.

A further point about the appearance of the poems on the page is that Mew cared a great deal about not having any of those lines of hers that are unusually long made to run over on to new lines. Quoting a letter to Harold Monro of 9 February 1916, in which Mew writes of how to manage 'the abnormal lines of "Madeleine" (which I am sure should not turn over)', Alida Monro comments: 'It was quite impossible to make her understand that certain exigencies of space prevented the printer, however much he might wish to carry out her directions, from having the lines the full width of the page' (CP p. xvii). With both *The Farmer's Bride* and *The Rambling Sailor* the Poetry Bookshop was seeking to avoid such run-ons or 'turn-overs' by giving the books an unusually wide format. Consequently, in 'The Fête', as printed by it, only two lines run on (the last two of the 8th stanza) and in 'Madeleine in Church' only four. Val Warner and Carcanet heed this concern of Mew's, in CPP by using smaller print for the poems than for the prose in the same volume and in CPSP by using for the poems a print-font in which the letters are exceptionally narrow. In CPSP only those same two lines run on in 'The

Fête' and only two in 'Madeleine in Church'. Perhaps some loss as well as the gain results from the narrow print, through the lines not looking as long as they are.

## V.R.I.

Three lines from the end of II, CPP and CPSP correct the 'lip' of the text printed in *Temple Bar* to 'lips'. But, in nineteenth-century 'poetical' style, Mew probably intended a dignified archaism with 'lip'. Tennyson uses 'lip' in a number of places, for example in 'The Gardener's Daughter': 'not less among us lived / Her fame from lip to lip'.

## Not for that City

*when all is said, all thought, all done,*: As first printed in *Temple Bar*. The final comma was replaced by a full stop from RS onwards, with lines 10 and 11 also less indented.

## Afternoon Tea

*tea with – the birds*: This dash is in a BL5 corrected typescript, not in other editions.

## The Farmer's Bride

The poem is punctuated as when first printed in *The Nation*. The only really significant difference from the punctuation in other editions is the one at the end of line 6 of the 1st stanza. 'Like the shut of a winter's day' has a full stop at the end in all the other editions except CP. (But it is also omitted in Christopher L. Carduff's selection of Mew poems printed in the US edition of Penelope Fitzgerald's biography *Charlotte Mew and her Friends*, 1988). I have followed the text in *The Nation* neither in its line-indentations, which differ in the 1st, 2nd and last stanzas, nor in its capitalizing of the first letters of 'harvest-time' and 'love' in the 1st stanza.

## Fame

*And the divine, wise trees that do not care*: The line ends with a full stop in *The New Weekly* and FB (1916). There is no punctuation at the end of this line in any of the other editions except CP, which has a comma.

### The Fête

For the text of this poem I have followed a Buffalo typescript, except in the cases noted below and in the many different line-indentations. (The latter can be seen in the text printed in the Appendix.) The text printed here differs from those in editions from *The Farmer's Bride* onwards in one piece of lineation (noted below), and in some punctuation and use of initial capital letters. Both in these latter respects and in its line-indentations the text of the Buffalo typescript differs a little less often from the text printed in *The Egoist*.

**1st stanza**

Both *moon*, in the two uses of the word in this stanza, and *wood* begin with capital letters in the Buffalo typescript.

*sacré*: The accent is missing from the typescript.

**4th stanza**

*sun's*: This word begins with a capital letter in the typescript.

*beyond the twinkling town*: As in the typescript and *Egoist*: this is a separate new line in other editions.

**5th stanza**

*Fair*: This is corrected, as in other editions, from the 'fair' of the typescript and *Egoist*. Both the latter have 'Fair' in the last line of the 9th stanza.

*montaine*: FB corrected Mew's French to *montagne*, but the typescript's spelling is retained here because the rhythm is affected. *The Egoist* printed *montane*.

*tir*: The word begins with a capital letter in the typescript.

*gaufres!*: All other editions substitute this for the '*quafres!*' of the typescript, *Egoist* and all three editions of FB.

*Ah! qu'elle est belle!*: This is a correction made by Mew herself to the '*Ah! que c'est belle!*' of the typescript and *Egoist*. (See the letter to Harold Monro of 18 January 1916, Davidow p. 314.)

**8th stanza**

*Oh! God it dies.*: 'Oh God! it dies,' in *Egoist* and other editions.

*But after death?*: As in the typescript and *Egoist*; 'But after death –,' other editions.

**11th stanza**

*Even unto you?*: The typescript and *Egoist* have 'Even to you?'.

### In Nunhead Cemetery

**8th stanza**
*But still it was a lovely thing*: This line and all of the poem that follows it are omitted without explanation from CP.

### The Pedlar

Punctuation is as in the poem as first printed in *The Englishwoman*, lighter in four places than in other editions.

### The Changeling

In a few places punctuation and line-indentation are different from those of other editions, following what is in the Buffalo corrected and signed typescript. In a small number of cases the different punctuation of this typescript is followed in *The Englishwoman* and FB (1916). The initial capital letters for 'Father', 'Mother' and 'Spring' in all previous editions are printed though they are not in this typescript, because they conform with Mew's normal practice.

### Ken

**1st stanza**
*black-clad*: This is not hyphenated in FB (1916, 1921).
*But in the morning*: FB (1916) has 'Though' instead of 'But'.

### The Forest Road

In a number of places the punctuation here differs from that of other editions, though less from that of FB (1916), following what is in a BL5 typescript. The most significant difference is in the line (thirteen from the end): 'If without waking you I could get up and reach the door –', where the other editions, except FB (1916), have an exclamation-mark after the dash at the end, as well as commas around 'without waking you'.

### On the Road to the Sea

In FB (1921), followed here by CPP and CPSP, there is no full stop at the end of the fifth stanza. But the full stop is there in *The Englishwoman* and also in the 3rd (1929) edition of FB and in CP.

### The Sunlit House

*Cared to go past it, night or day,*: In FB and CPP the first of the two commas comes between 'past' and 'it', clearly by mistake. It is simply omitted in CP and CPSP.

### Song ('Love Love to-day, my dear')

The punctuation is lighter here than in other editions (though with a full stop instead of a semi-colon at the end of each stanza's line 4), following a Berg manuscript.

### Saturday Market

The punctuation is as in a Buffalo manuscript. For that manuscript's very different line-indentations see the text of the poem in the Appendix. In the manuscript it is 'on' – not 'in' – 'a kind old tree' in line 2, but here I follow the editions from FB onwards.

### Sea Love

Buffalo has two manuscripts, one a corrected manuscript and with the line-indentations like those in the poem as first printed in *The Chapbook* (except that line 8 is less indented than in *The Chapbook*, where its indentation is the same as line 4's), and a second manuscript that appears to be Mew's fair copy, slightly changed, of the corrected one. The punctuation of the fair copy is followed here. But it is not impossible that Mew made this fair copy after the poem had been printed, or that then her lighter punctuation of its second stanza was casual and not a deliberate change. The text of that corrected manuscript is given in the Appendix.

*Heer's the same*: 'Here's the same' in the Buffalo 'fair copy' ms.

### The Road to Kérity

The punctuation is as in a BL5 typescript, which also has the centring of the poem's last two lines (as against their position far over to the right in all other editions).

### *I Have Been Through the Gates*

The punctuation is as in the poem's first printing in *The Chapbook*. Buffalo has both a corrected typescript and Mew's corrected proof for *The Chapbook*.

### *The Cenotaph*

As in *The Westminster Gazette*. From FB (1921) onwards a few commas were added.

### *The Wheat*

In CPP and CPSP extra space is left after paragraphs 1, 3, 6, 10, 12, 15 and 22. In the BL4 corrected typescript the extra space comes after paragraphs 1, possibly 3 (but not certainly, since the typescript goes on to a new page here), 10, 14 and 15. The present edition follows the typescript, as also in punctuation. See this edition's other Notes for a record of the ms. alterations Mew made on this typescript.

### *Rooms*

The punctuation and line-indentations are as in a BL5 corrected typescript.
*As we shall some day*: BL5 typescript; other editions: 'As we shall somewhere'.
*the other dustier quieter bed*: BL5 typescript; other editions: 'the other quieter, dustier bed'.
*Out there – in the sun –*: The first dash in this line is not in other editions, only in the BL5 typescript.

### *Monsieur Qui Passe*

The punctuation is as in a corrected BL5 typescript.

### *Again*

The punctuation is as in a corrected Buffalo typescript, lighter than in other editions.

### *I so liked Spring*

The punctuation is as in a corrected typescript in BL5.

### May, *1915*

In line 2, 'all' is in a BL5 corrected typescript, but not in other editions, as also the absence of a comma at the end of line 6. For this typescript's different line-indentations see the text in the Appendix.

### Ne Me Tangito

Punctuation and line-indentations differ slightly from those of other editions, following those in a BL5 typescript.

### The Rambling Sailor

The punctuation is as when the poem was first printed in *The Chapbook*, a little lighter than in other editions.

### Moorland Night

The punctuation and line-indentations are as in a Buffalo typescript, only a little different from those of the poem as first printed in *The Nation and the Athenaeum*, more different from those of other editions.

### Appendix

In this text of *The Fête* the line-indentations are as in a Buffalo typescript. These texts of *Saturday Market*, *Sea Love* and *May*, *1915* are as in, respectively, a Buffalo manuscript, a Buffalo corrected manuscript and a BL5 typescript. But that manuscript of 'Sea Love' has 'everlasting' instead of 'everlastin'' in line 4.

# Index of Titles

Absence 85
A Farewell 4
Afternoon Tea 9
Again 75
An Ending 88
A Question 3
A Quoi Bon Dire 36
Arracombe Wood 59
At the Convent Gate 7

Beside the Bed 25

Do Dreams Lie Deeper? 73
Domus Caedet Arborem 74

Epitaph 75
Exspecto Resurrectionem 50

Fame 18
Fin de Fête 74
Friends, Wherefore –? 76
From a Window 71

Here Lies a Prisoner 77

I Have Been Through the Gates 60
In Nunhead Cemetery 25
In the Fields 71
I so liked Spring 76

Jour des Morts 39
June, 1915 77

Ken 33

Left Behind 4
Le Sacré-Coeur 56

Madeleine in Church 42
May, 1915 77, 98
Monsieur Qui Passe 72
Moorland Night 87
My Heart is Lame 80

Ne Me Tangito 78
Not for that City 9

Old Shepherd's Prayer 79
On the Asylum Road 39
On the Road to the Sea 53
On Youth Struck Down 80

Pécheresse 29
Péri en Mer 13

Requiescat 11
Rooms 72

Saturday Market 57, 96
Sea Love 59, 97

She was a Sinner 13
Smile, Death 82
Song ('Love Love today, my dear')
    57
Song ('Oh! Sorrow, Sorrow, scarce I
    knew') 8

The Call 84
The Cenotaph 61
The Changeling 31
The Farmer's Bride 17
The Féte 20, 91
The Forest Road 40
The Little Portress 10

The Narrow Door 19
The Pedlar 28
The Quiet House 36
The Rambling Sailor 83
'There shall be no night there' 3
The Road to Kérity 60
The Shade-Catchers
The Sunlit House 55
The Trees are Down 81
The Wheat 65
To a Child in Death 86
To a Little Child in Death 6

V.R.I. 5

# Index of First Lines

Across these wind-blown meadows I can see 3
'A Nation's Sorrow.' No. In that strange hour 5
A purple blot against the dead white door 72

Bury your heart in some deep green hollow 57, 96

Dear, if little feet make little journeys, 6
'DON'T LET them cut the Wheat' he had said, 65
Down the long quay the slow boats glide, 29
Do you remember the two old people we passed on the road to Kérity, 60

Ever since the great planes were murdered at the end of the gardens 74

From our low seat beside the fire 84

He loved gay things 75
Here, in the darkness, where this plaster saint 42
His dust looks up to the changing sky 73
His heart, to me, was a place of palaces and pinnacles and shining towers; 60

If Christ was crucified – Ah! God, are we 3
In the old back streets o' Pimlico 83
I remember rooms that have had their part 72
I so liked Spring last year 76
I think they were about as high 55
It is dark up here on the heights, 56
It is the clay that makes the earth stick to his spade;
I will not count the years – there are days too – 76

Leave him: he's quiet enough: and what matter 77
Lend me a little while the key 28
Let us remember Spring will come again 77, 98
Lord, when I look at lovely things which pass, 71
Love Love today, my dear 57
Love was my flower, and before He came – 13

My face is against the grass – the moorland grass is wet – 87
My heart is lame with running after yours so fast 80

Not for that city of the level sun, 9
Not yet will those measureless fields be green again 61

Odd, *You* should fear the touch, 78
Oh, Death what have you to say? 80
Oh! King who hast the key 50
Oh! Sorrow, Sorrow, scarce I knew 8
One day, not here, you will find a hand 75
One day the friends who stand about my bed 13

Please you, excuse me, good five o'clock people, 9

Remember me and smile, as smiling too, 4

Seventeen years ago you said 36
Smile, Death, see I smile as I come to you 82
Someone has shut the shining eyes, straightened and folded 25
Some said, because he wudn' spaik 59
Sometimes I know the way 85
Sometimes in the over-heated house, but not for long, 18
Sweetheart, for such a day 74
Sweetheart, is this the last of all our posies 39

The forest road, 40
Theirs is the house whose windows – every pane – 39
The narrow door, the narrow door 19
The stillness of the sunshine lies 10
The town is old and very steep, 33
They are cutting down the great plane-trees at the end of the gardens. 81
Three Summers since I chose a maid – 17

Tide be runnin' the great world over; 59, 97
Toll no bell for me, dear Father, dear Mother, 31
To-night again the moon's white mat 20, 91

Up here, with June, the sycamore throws 71
Up to the bed by the window, where I be lyin', 79

We passed each other, turned and stopped for half an hour, then went our
    way, 53
When we were children old Nurse used to say, 36
When, wrapped in the calm majesty of sleep, 6
White through the gate it gleamed and slept 55
Who thinks of June's first rose to-day? 77
'Why do you shrink away, and start and stare? – 7
Wilt thou have pity? intercede for me. 4

You know that road beside the sea, 88
You would have scoffed if we had told you yesterday 86
Your birds that call from tree to tree 11

# PENGUIN (🐧) CLASSICS

## www.penguinclassics.com

- Details about every Penguin Classic

- Advanced information about forthcoming titles

- Hundreds of author biographies

- FREE resources including critical essays on the books and their historical background, reader's and teacher's guides.

- Links to other web resources for the Classics

- Discussion area

- Online review copy ordering for academics

- Competitions with prizes, and challenging Classics trivia quizzes

# READ MORE IN PENGUIN

In every corner of the world, on every subject under the sun, Penguin represents quality and variety – the very best in publishing today.

For complete information about books available from Penguin – including Puffins, Penguin Classics and Arkana – and how to order them, write to us at the appropriate address below. Please note that for copyright reasons the selection of books varies from country to country.

**In the United Kingdom**: Please write to *Dept. EP, Penguin Books Ltd, Bath Road, Harmondsworth, West Drayton, Middlesex UB7 ODA*

**In the United States**: Please write to *Consumer Sales, Penguin Putnam Inc., P.O. Box 12289 Dept. B, Newark, New Jersey 07101-5289*. VISA and MasterCard holders call 1-800-788-6262 to order Penguin titles

**In Canada**: Please write to *Penguin Books Canada Ltd, 10 Alcorn Avenue, Suite 300, Toronto, Ontario M4V 3B2*

**In Australia**: Please write to *Penguin Books Australia Ltd, P.O. Box 257, Ringwood, Victoria 3134*

**In New Zealand**: Please write to *Penguin Books (NZ) Ltd, Private Bag 102902, North Shore Mail Centre, Auckland 10*

**In India**: Please write to *Penguin Books India Pvt Ltd, 11 Community Centre, Panchsheel Park, New Delhi 110017*

**In the Netherlands**: Please write to *Penguin Books Netherlands bv, Postbus 3507, NL-1001 AH Amsterdam*

**In Germany**: Please write to *Penguin Books Deutschland GmbH, Metzlerstrasse 26, 60594 Frankfurt am Main*

**In Spain**: Please write to *Penguin Books S. A., Bravo Murillo 19, 1° B, 28015 Madrid*

**In Italy**: Please write to *Penguin Italia s.r.l., Via Benedetto Croce 2, 20094 Corsico, Milano*

**In France**: Please write to *Penguin France, Le Carré Wilson, 62 rue Benjamin Baillaud, 31500 Toulouse*

**In Japan**: Please write to *Penguin Books Japan Ltd, Kaneko Building, 2-3-25 Koraku, Bunkyo-Ku, Tokyo 112*

**In South Africa**: Please write to *Penguin Books South Africa (Pty) Ltd, Private Bag X14, Parkview, 2122 Johannesburg*

# READ MORE IN PENGUIN

*Published or forthcoming:*

**Ulysses**  James Joyce

Written over a seven-year period, from 1914 to 1921, *Ulysses* has survived bowdlerization, legal action and bitter controversy. An undisputed modernist classic, its ceaseless verbal inventiveness and astonishingly wide-ranging allusions confirm its standing as an imperishable monument to the human condition. 'Everybody knows now that *Ulysses* is the greatest novel of the century' Anthony Burgess, *Observer*

**Nineteen Eighty-Four**  George Orwell

Hidden away in the Record Department of the Ministry of Truth, Winston Smith skilfully rewrites the past to suit the needs of the Party. Yet he inwardly rebels against the totalitarian world he lives in, which controls him through the all-seeing eye of Big Brother. 'His final masterpiece . . . *Nineteen Eighty-Four* is enthralling' Timothy Garton Ash, *New York Review of Books*

**The Day of the Locust *and* The Dream Life of Balso Snell**
Nathanael West

These two novellas demonstrate the fragility of the American dream. In *The Day of the Locust*, talented young artist Todd Hackett has been brought to Hollywood to work in a major studio. He discovers a surreal world of tarnished dreams, where violence and hysteria lurk behind the glittering façade. 'The best of the Hollywood novels, a nightmare vision of humanity destroyed by its obsession with film' J. G. Ballard, *Sunday Times*

**The Myth of Sisyphus**  Albert Camus

*The Myth of Sisyphus* is one of the most profound philosophical statements written this century. It is a discussion of the central idea of absurdity that Camus was to develop in his novel *The Outsider*. Here Camus poses the fundamental question – Is life worth living? – and movingly argues for an acceptance of reality that encompasses revolt, passion and, above all, liberty.

# READ MORE IN PENGUIN

*Published or forthcoming:*

**The Diary of a Young Girl**   Anne Frank

This definitive edition of Anne Frank's diary restores substantial material omitted from the original edition, giving us a deeper insight into her world. 'One of the greatest books of the twentieth century . . . If you have never read Anne Frank's diary, or haven't read it for years, this is the edition to buy' *Guardian*

**Brideshead Revisited**   Evelyn Waugh

The most nostalgic of Evelyn Waugh's novels, *Brideshead Revisited* looks back to the golden age before the Second World War. It tells the story of Charles Ryder's infatuation with the Marchmains and the rapidly disappearing world of privilege they inhabit. 'Lush and evocative . . . expresses at once the profundity of change and the indomitable endurance of the human spirit' *The Times*

**Oranges**   John McPhee

From Thailand, where the sweetest oranges are as green as emeralds, to Florida oranges so juicy it is said they should be peeled in the bath, the orange exists in bounteous varieties. John McPhee has woven together history, anecdote and science to create a definitive guide to the world of oranges. 'A classic of American reportage. McPhee is quirky, original and intensely curious' Julian Barnes

**Wide Sargasso Sea**   Jean Rhys

Inspired by Charlotte Brontë's *Jane Eyre*, *Wide Sargasso Sea* is set in the lush landscape of Jamaica in the 1830s. Born into an oppressive colonialist society, Creole heiress Antoinette Cosway meets and marries a young Englishman. But as Antoinette becomes caught between his demands and her own precarious sense of belonging, she is eventually driven towards madness.

# READ MORE IN PENGUIN

*Published or forthcoming:*

**Love in a Cold Climate and Other Novels**  Nancy Mitford

Nancy Mitford's brilliantly witty, irreverent stories of the upper classes in pre-war London and Paris conjure up a world of glamour and decadence, in which her heroines deal with hilariously eccentric relatives, the excitement of love and passion, and the thrills of the Season. But beneath their glittering surfaces, Nancy Mitford's novels are also hymns to a lost era and to the brevity of life and love.

**The Prime of Miss Jean Brodie**  Muriel Spark

Romantic, heroic, comic and tragic, schoolmistress Jean Brodie has become an iconic figure in post-war fiction. Her glamour, freethinking ideas and manipulative charm hold dangerous sway over her girls at the Marcia Blaine Academy, who are introduced to a privileged world of adult games that they will never forget. 'A sublimely funny book . . . unforgettable and universal'  Candia McWilliam

**Sons and Lovers**  D. H. Lawrence

Gertrude Morel, a delicate yet determined woman, no longer loves her boorish husband and devotes herself to her sons, William and Paul. Inevitably there is conflict when Paul falls in love and seeks to escape his mother's grasp. Lawrence's modern masterpiece reflects the transition between the past and the future, between one generation and the next, and between childhood and adolescence.

**Cold Comfort Farm**  Stella Gibbons

When the sukebind is in the bud, orphaned, expensively educated Flora Poste descends on her relatives at Cold Comfort Farm. There are plenty of them – Amos, called by God; Seth, smouldering with sex; and, of course, Great Aunt Ada Doom, who saw 'something nasty in the woodshed' . . . 'Very probably the funniest book ever written' Julie Burchill, *Sunday Times*

# READ MORE IN PENGUIN

*Published or forthcoming:*

**A Confederacy of Dunces**   John Kennedy Toole

A monument to sloth, rant and contempt, a behemoth of fat, flatulence and furious suspicion of anything modern – this is Ignatius J. Reilly of New Orleans. In magnificent revolt against the twentieth century, he propels his monstrous bulk among the flesh-pots of a fallen city, a noble crusader against a world of dunces. 'A masterwork of comedy' *The New York Times*

**Giovanni's Room**   James Baldwin

Set in the bohemian world of 1950s Paris, *Giovanni's Room* is a landmark in gay writing. David is casually introduced to a barman named Giovanni and stays overnight with him. One night lengthens to more than three months of covert passion in his room. As he waits for his fiancée to arrive from Spain, David idealizes his planned marriage while tragically failing to see Giovanni's real love.

**Breakfast at Tiffany's**   Truman Capote

It's New York in the 1940s, where the Martinis flow from cocktail-hour to breakfast at Tiffany's. And nice girls don't, except, of course, Holly Golightly. Pursued by Mafia gangsters and playboy millionaires, Holly is a fragile eyeful of tawny hair and turned-up nose. She is irrepressibly 'top banana in the shock department', and one of the shining flowers of American fiction.

**Delta of Venus**   Anaïs Nin

In *Delta of Venus* Anaïs Nin conjures up a glittering cascade of sexual encounters. Creating her own 'language of the senses', she explores an area that was previously the domain of male writers and brings to it her own unique perceptions. Her vibrant and impassioned prose evokes the essence of female sexuality in a world where only love has meaning.

# READ MORE IN PENGUIN

*Published or forthcoming:*

**The Chrysalids**  John Wyndham

Genetic mutation has devastated the world. In the primitive society that has emerged from its ruins, any sign of deviation is ruthlessly hunted out and destroyed. David lives in fear of discovery, for he is part of a secret group who are able to communicate with each other through their thoughts. As they grow older they feel increasingly isolated. Then one of them marries a 'norm' with terrifying consequences.

**The Waves**  Virginia Woolf

*The Waves* traces the lives of a group of friends from childhood to youth and middle age. While social events, individual achievements and disappointments form its narrative, the novel is most remarkable for the poetic language that conveys the inner life of its characters: their aspirations, their triumphs and regrets, their awareness of unity and isolation.

**Heart of Darkness**  Joseph Conrad

In Conrad's haunting tale Marlow, a seaman and wanderer, recounts his journey to the heart of Africa in search of the enigmatic Kurtz. He discovers how Kurtz has gained his position of power over the local people, and radically questions not only his own nature and values, but those of his society. '*Heart of Darkness* seemed to reach into the heart of Conrad himself' Peter Ackroyd, *The Times*

**The Garden Party and Other Stories**  Katherine Mansfield

Innovative, startlingly perceptive and aglow with colour, these fifteen stories were written towards the end of Katherine Mansfield's short life. Many are set in the author's native New Zealand, others in England and the French Riviera. All are revelations of the unspoken, half-understood emotions that make up everyday experience.

# READ MORE IN PENGUIN

*Published or forthcoming:*

**Seven Pillars of Wisdom**  T. E. Lawrence

Although 'continually and bitterly ashamed' that the Arabs had risen in revolt against the Turks as a result of fraudulent British promises, Lawrence led them in a triumphant campaign. *Seven Pillars of Wisdom* recreates epic events with extraordinary vividness. However flawed, Lawrence is one of the twentieth century's most fascinating figures. This is the greatest monument to his character.

**A Month in the Country**  J. L. Carr

A damaged survivor of the First World War, Tom Birkin finds refuge in the village church of Oxgodby where he is to spend the summer uncovering a huge medieval wall-painting. Immersed in the peace of the countryside and the unchanging rhythms of village life, Birkin experiences a sense of renewal. Now an old man, he looks back on that idyllic summer of 1920.

**Lucky Jim**  Kingsley Amis

Jim Dixon has accidentally fallen into a job at one of Britain's new redbrick universities. A moderately successful future beckons, as long as he can survive a madrigal-singing weekend at Professor Welch's, deliver a lecture on 'Merrie England' and resist Christine, the hopelessly desirable girlfriend of Welch's awful son Bertrand. 'A flawless comic novel . . . It has always made me laugh out loud' Helen Dunmore, *The Times*

**Under Milk Wood**  Dylan Thomas

As the inhabitants of Llareggub lie sleeping, their dreams and fantasies deliciously unfold. Waking up, their dreams turn to bustling activity as a new day begins. In this classic modern pastoral, the 'dismays and rainbows' of the imagined seaside town become, within the cycle of one day, 'a greenleaved sermon on the innocence of men'.

# READ MORE IN PENGUIN

*Published or forthcoming:*

**Swann's Way**  Marcel Proust

This first book of Proust's supreme masterpiece, *A la recherche du temps perdu*, recalls the early youth of Charles Swann in the small, provincial backwater of Combray through the eyes of the adult narrator. The story then moves forward to Swann's life as a man of fashion in the glittering world of *belle-époque* Paris. A scathing, often comic dissection of French society, *Swann's Way* is also a story of past moments tantalizingly lost and, finally, triumphantly rediscovered.

**Metamorphosis and Other Stories**  Franz Kafka

A companion volume to *The Great Wall of China and Other Short Works*, these translations bring together the small proportion of Kafka's works that he thought worthy of publication. This volume contains his most famous story, 'Metamorphosis'. All the stories reveal the breadth of Kafka's literary vision and the extraordinary imaginative depth of his thought.

**Cancer Ward**  Aleksandr Solzhenitsyn

One of the great allegorical masterpieces of world literature, *Cancer Ward* is both a deeply compassionate study of people facing terminal illness and a brilliant dissection of the 'cancerous' Soviet police state. Withdrawn from publication in Russia in 1964, it became a work that awoke the conscience of the world. 'Without doubt the greatest Russian novelist of this century' *Sunday Times*

**Peter Camenzind**  Hermann Hesse

In a moment of 'emotion recollected in tranquility' Peter Camenzind recounts the days of his youth: his childhood in a remote mountain village, his abiding love of nature, and the discovery of literature which inspires him to leave the village and become a writer. 'One of the most penetrating accounts of a young man trying to discover the nature of his creative talent' *The Times Literary Supplement*